THE
COMPLEAT
WATERFOWLER

Other outdoor books by B. R. Peterson

The Original Roadkill Cookbook
Buck Peterson's Complete Guide to Deer Hunting
Buck Peterson's Complete Guide to Fishing
Buck Peterson's Complete Guide to Indoor Life
The Endangered Species Cookbook
The International Roadkill Cookbook

THE COMPLEAT WATERFOWLER

A Discourse on Duck Hunting
with a
Little Goose on the Side

B.R. "BUCK" PETERSON

ILLUSTRATIONS BY J. ANGUS "SOURDOUGH" McLEAN

THE LYONS PRESS
Guilford, Connecticut
An imprint of The Globe Pequot Press

DISCLAIMER
Buck and other responsible bird biologists are expanding the limits of avian research so rapidly that the scientific information contained in the text might be outdated by the time you reach the distinguished author photo in the back. For that reason (and a nudge by the libel and slander attorneys holding the publisher hostage), Buck takes no responsibility for the accuracy or, for that matter, the necessity of most of this material.

The Lyons Press is an imprint of The Globe Pequot Press.

10 9 8 7 6 5 4 3 2 1

Manufactured in the United States of America

ISBN: 1-58574-776-9

Library of Congress Cataloging-in-Publication data is available on file.

For Kim Peterson,
the best of duck hunting pals,
and Gregory and Matthew

CONTENTS

ACKNOWLEDGMENTS

No outdoor humor book can avoid a large debt to the late Ed Zern and his distinguished career of making outdoor stuff fun (and whose earlier work would make Buck's material seem relatively tame). *Ducks, Geese and Swans of North America* by Francis H. Kortright, John C. Philips's *A Natural History of the Ducks*, Frank C. Bellrose's *Ducks, Geese and Swans of North America*, Ernest A. Choate's *Dictionary Of American Bird Names*, Steve Madge and Hilary Burn's *Waterfowl*, and any work on waterfowl by Paul A. Johnsgard are great places to learn more about ducks. Owning a pig, any pig, is the only way to appreciate Dorothy's contribution to the sport.

Thanks to Eli and Wendell for their advice on duck calls, Sam for duck clubs, decoys, and a homeboy goose hunt, Frank for the last day of the season on the salt marsh, and Richard for his enthusiasm for all things wild. Thanks also to the hardworking duck specialists of the U.S. Fish and Wildlife Service, Environment Canada, and Ducks Unlimited.

Irreverence for all things too serious is shared by Buck's co-conspirator and good buddy, J. Angus "Sourdough" McLean. An

"SOURDOUGH"

old marsh rat like Buck, "Sourdough" is a true sportsman and a good sport, and his fine illustrations expand and refresh the tradition of sporting art. Waterfowlers are the best kind of people and "Sourdough" is the best kind of waterfowler.

INTRODUCKTION

Buck's first memories of Minnesota duck hunting involved competition for "the point," a small spit of land that poked its nose into the middle of a crescent-shaped lake. Any ducks in the area would move from one end of the lake to the other over a scraggly patch of marsh grass and cattail at the end of this sand spit. The lake was less than five miles from town and all a couple of teenagers had to do to hunt ducks was leave home early enough in the morning, stash the dark blue '55 Ford pickup, crawl under (or risk the soft Red Ball waders going over) the barbed wire fence, and walk quietly through the scrub oak woods above the shoreline hoping nobody beat them to the best natural blind on the lake. If the point was occupied, Buck and his high school hunting buddy sat in the ditch along the road that separated the crescent-shaped lake from others for a pass-shot at ducks already in high gear. That first lake served the cause until another, more private lake to the north was found that worked equally well for catching turtles on a hot summer afternoon. As measured in paraphernalia, it was on that nameless second lake that Buck's duck hunting skills came into play with handmade wooden decoys bobbing in front of a natural cattail blind and a Herter's canoe handy to retrieve whatever fell from the sky.

In those early days, waterfowling was first an extension of friendship with a brother-in-law to be, and then a family affair carving and painting decoys in the basement and hot-waxing ducks out in the garage. The traditions have continued over the years as a heady brew of family and friends has floated and jump-shot the Snake River, flushed

bluebills out of irrigation ponds, and tried to stomp the cold out of a
goose pit while waiting for the big honkers to come off the Columbia
River for the morning feed.

   . Above all, waterfowling must be a passion for the ducks. *The
Compleat Waterfowler* is for all the marsh rats who share this passion,
particularly those who have shared Buck's blind. It is different from
other waterfowling books in that it is neither only this or that nor here
or there, with the exception of black and white copy, which can be
blamed on Buck who sees sportsman's ethics in those designer shades of
gray. *The Compleat Waterfowler* is actually the first book for the duck
blind. The chapters on the duck are chock full of respect for Buck's little duck-billed buddies and are placed in the front of the book for the
front of the reader's attention. Those who hunt with Buck have memo-
rized the extraordinary detail of the chapter on species identification
and recommend that conservation organizations offer this chapter to
their members as a public service. To bypass cumbersome publisher
agreements, copyright releases and direct deposit slips to Buck's personal
checking account have been sent to these groups as a private service.

   The section on the duck hunt is predictably engorged with solid recommendations on essential gear and, at great personal risk, the straight
skinny on the canine/retriever conspiracies. In all likelihood, the information on hunting creates the first print version of blind virtual reality,
an actual day in the forward artillery posts of Big Babe Lake. The book is
the operations bible at Buck's Duck Hunting Lodge in northernmost
Minnesota, and a most sincere token of appreciation to all serious waterfowlers from Buck, director of etiquette of the Dead Duck Society, and
Dorothy, his champion hunting pig.

ON THE WINGS OF A SNOW WHITE GOOSE
(Anthem of the Dead Duck Society)

At the wings of a snow white goose (goose sounds)
We send our steel shot loose.
A double barrel sluice
At the wings of a goose.

When the office surrounds us
When bossmen come
The spirit grows weak
The body grows dumb.

When this stuff upsets us
Birds don't forget us.
They send down a goose
We let steel shot loose.

At the wings of a snow white goose
We send our steel shot loose.
A double barrel sluice
At the wings of a goose.

When Buck had drifted
In the marsh many days
He searched for birds
That wouldn't stray.

Troubles he had some
But he forgot them.
From the sky came his goose
He let steel shot loose.

At the wings of a snow white goose (shotgun sounds)
We send our steel shot loose
A double barreled sluice
At the wings of a goose.

At the wings of a snow white goose
We send our steel shot loose.
A double barreled sluice
At the wings of a goose.

At the wings of a goose.
At the wings of a goose.
At the wings of a goose.

(sung to the tune of Ferlin Husky's "On the Wings of a Dove")

TOP TEN QUESTIONS ABOUT DUCK HUNTING

Dear Buck: Did ducks always quack?

No. The first ducks didn't make any noise. These pioneer ducks were, however, very impressionable and learned to imitate the pioneer hunters that amused their buddies with funny noises created from pockets of air in their face cheeks and elsewhere. Ducks born in the South sound more like heavy cloth ripping. Canadian birds sound much like the opening of a beer can.

Dear Buck: Do ducks and geese have a God?

Yes. The inventor of steel shot.

Dear Buck: Does the American Dental Association have a God?

Yes. The inventor of steel shot.

Dear Buck: Do migrating ducks suffer from jet lag?

Yes. But experienced long-distance fliers, such as the blue-winged teal, prevent the obvious distress caused by the interruption of the body's circadian rhythm by avoiding in-flight alcoholic drinks and not sleeping immediately after landing.

Dear Buck: Is it true that the U.S. Air Force is secretly training and using bomb-equipped "smart ducks" in combat?

Maybe. Off the record, some sources confide that it's easier than teaching the navy's dolphins to fly.

Dear Buck: Do ducks go to the bathroom, you know, toilet, you know, number one or two, when they are flying? If so, you know, how?

Yes, you know. They are supposed to ask for permission to leave the formation. Those who don't are never asked back.

Dear Buck: If a duck is born in Canada yet is shot over Minnesota, does the successful duck hunter have to drink Canadian beer?

No one should have to do that! If a duck born in Canada is shot over Wisconsin, which is unlikely, beer brewed in Wisconsin is not recommended either. For any occasion.

Dear Buck: When you measure fingers of bourbon, is it okay to use any finger?

Yes. If you're partaking of a more boastful waterfowler's finest malt beverage, thumbs up.

Dear Buck: What's the deal with water off a duck's back? Like, if I turned a fire hose on one of those dumb-looking mallards in the park, would that be too much water?

No.

Dear Buck: Why is one leg of a V formation longer than another?

More birds.

PART ONE

THE DUCK

CHAPTER 1

EVOLUTION OF THE DUCK

T o the possible surprise of a few marsh rats, ducks belong to the bird family, not the other way around, and the first ducks are found in the big bird family album.

Birds appeared on earth near the end of the Jurassic period, over 150 million years ago. These pilgrims preferred not to fly freely until the flying predator reptiles or pterosaurs were permanently grounded about sixty-four million years ago.

The very first bird is thought to be the Archaeopteryx, Latin for "ancient wing or feather." It evolved from some sort of dinosaur with birdlike primary and secondary asymmetrical flight feathers and symmetrical tail feathers, with a beaked face full of sharp teeth and claws on its "fingers" like a reptile.

The Archaeopteryx did not have typical bird flight muscles and is thought to have been more like a glider that would climb to the top of a tree and fall off (much like the old fossil tree stand deer hunters of Wisconsin). Scientists refer to this ancient bird fossil found in the warm malt swamps of Bavaria in 1861 as a solid evolutionary link between dinosaurs and

ARCHAEOPTERYX

birds. However, most waterfowlers have adopted the duckbill dinosaurs or "hadrosaurs" as the significant missing links.

DUCKBILL DINOSAURS

Three specific examples belong to one of two major orders of dinosaurs called the Ornithischia, or "bird-hipped," for the two lower hipbones lying together behind the back leg. Those paid less than union scale in period theme parks belong to the Saurischia or "lizard-hipped" order.

ANATOSAURUS

CORYTHOSAURUS

The unusual long-tailed Anatosaurus used its broad beak to scoop up vegetation. The Parasaurolophus had a distinctive long horn that was used to honk. With a butter plate stuck on its head, the Corythosaurus looks much like the modern crested duck.

There is solid fossil evidence that ducks and geese have existed in their present form for over fifty million years. These primitive ducks used to migrate by walking from their breeding grounds to their nesting areas along an ancient central route that would take two to three years. Although the walkway created by this migration has since been paved, contemporary migration memories are still triggered by the north-to-south federal highway system. This mid-American walkway had the largest concentration of waterfowl much to the disappointment of the early Pilgrims and most chambers of commerce along the yet-to-be-discovered Atlantic Flyway.

PARASAUROLOPHUS

ICHTHYORNIS

HESPERORNIS

Remnants of three of the more modern ducks have been found in the ancient central walkway. Two of the birds were found in the Midwest, one a gull- or ternlike bird with small but powerful wings called an Ichthyornis or "fish bird" and the second a five-foot-long loonlike diver named the Hesperornis or "western bird," with wings much too small to fly.

ACER PETERSORNIS

The third and ornithologically most significant duck fossil was found not too far south of Buck's Duck Hunting Lodge near where the now famous Kensington runestone was discovered. The first game bird of record, this ancient magnum mallard was distinguished by its Nordic warrior demeanor.

This magnificent specimen was reportedly slain by the exploring Vikings who inscribed the runestone. Cryptographers on the last two bar stools in the Valhalla Lounge have cracked the ancient code like a pickled hard-boiled egg and agree that the marks on the stone read much like the first duck hunt.

Translation: "To dozxen Goths tri snek up net big buk duck. Big fiiit. Won Goth left. Not feel good. Big duk dead. Good tink to. Tri make luteduck. Mis Olga. No minke whale to kill Big Babe Lake. Mis Lena to. Now lye down dye. Bye bye. Hav nis da. Sven."

CHAPTER 2

DUCK ANATOMY

The contemporary wild duck is a biological marvel and, unlike its domestic dolt relatives, is at the top of the evolutionary scale. To better understand how a duck works, the following duck parts have been thoroughly analyzed (and some eaten) by the scientists of Buck's Avian Research and Advanced Plucking Center.

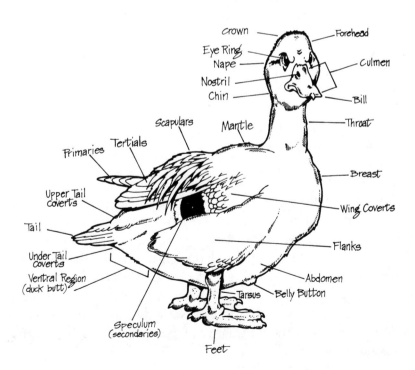

EYES

With eyes on both sides of the head, ducks can see a much larger area than we can; their fields of vision overlap in front and over the tops of their little pointy heads. Duck eyes see motion and create depth perception by comparing related motion at different distances. Their eyeballs have greater distances between the retina and lens than those of us mammals, allowing the image on the retina to broaden and sharpen so the bird can see better and farther. Duck eyes are also lined with cones and rods to distinguish the colors of inappropriate camouflage patterns under low-light conditions. Although research on duck vision has been concentrated on the mallard, it's assumed that all ducks are able to distinguish the three primary colors and may be able to see into the ultraviolet part of the spectrum, making it possible for them to see through the ground artillery smoke around Big Babe Lake.

EARS

A duck doesn't have ears like us. Loose feathers called "auricular" conceal ear holes, making earrings out of the question unless you are talking about the ear ringing produced by a 10-gauge magnum. A duck's inner ear functions much like ours but varies in size and shape by species.

When ducks don't seem to hear your call, it may be because they are hard of hearing or they know it's only you. All birds are most sensitive to sounds in the 1 to 5 kilohertz frequency range (1 kilohertz equals 1,000 vibrations per second). A duck's range of hearing is good enough to hear a muzzle blast and the untimely splashdown of a comrade. To compare ear holes, a young Buckster can hear sounds of up to 18 kilohertz. An old Buck hears only what he wants to.

BILL

Most duck bills or beaks are wide and flat. If your duck's bill is long and thin with a serrated edge, you've shot a merganser. Bon appétit! Duck nose parts are incorporated into the upper half of the beak. Most bills have hooks or "nails" at the end; the larger beaks are designed to dig mollusks. Marine species or diving ducks have enlarged nasal or salt glands located in the upper orbit of the eye that regulate the salt content in their blood. The salt is removed as a waste fluid that dribbles out the nostrils on the bill. If the nostrils get plugged at night, a multipurpose decongestant helps.

It's hard to know if ducks smell. They sure do if they're left to hang too long. But whether they can use their noses as humans do is uncertain. Divers certainly can't smell their food underwater. Can ducks smell their way along a migration route? A yes answer would explain how pintails draw a bearing on Los Angeles, California, and Tacoma, Washington. In certain parts of the country, the flap of skin that covers the duck butt is called the preacher's (or pope's) nose. This nose does not smell unless its owner has been eating asparagus.

MOUTH

Ducks taste good but are they good at tasting? It's not known whether a fat midwestern mallard prefers the taste of field corn over sweet corn; until farmers start spraying their crops with butter instead of salted water we'll never know. The few taste buds ducks have are in the roof of their mouth and their throat. Since they can't taste food, ducks don't spend much time chewing their food, and since they don't have to chew food, they have no need for real teeth, which keeps the flock's dental bills down, especially important in those marshlands that aren't fluoridated.

Ducks have soft, pink tongues that suck food into the front of the beak and expel water through the base between the mandibles. Ducks are not able to stick out their tongues at nonresident shooters unless they first pull the sides of their mouths back with their primary feathers.

Duck doctors have an awful time trying to do physicals on ducks as they will not keep a thermometer in their beak. Avian botulism, cholera, and duck virus enteritis are killers and the marsh medics need to know whether the bird's temperature is a normal 109 degrees.

To find where the quack comes from, you need to force open the mouth of a drake mallard and look down the gullet for the duck call, called the syrinx, a bony enlargement at the base of the trachea. The syrinx is a resonating chamber with thin walls of elastic, vibrating membranes that can modify a quack to a whistlelike note. Specialized muscles control the movement of the syrinx including the tension on the membranes. Both intensity (loudness) and frequency (pitch) can be altered by varying the pressure of the air passing from the lungs and the tension exerted by syringeal muscles on the membranes. Note that the syrinx is not made of an exotic hardwood. Hens have a very simple trachea and if you hear a quack, it's likely to be a female.

Do ducks talk or sing? There is little noted musical quality in duck talk. Can ducks create a series of notes in a barely cohesive sequence like an Irish tenor in the wee hours of the morning? No! Do ducks have a swan song? Yes! It's sung by *any* drake mallard flying in range of Buck's blind.

BRAIN

Duck quackpersons disavow the term *bird brain* but that is not to say some birds aren't smarter than others. Not at all. Wildfowl are smarter than domestic fowl. The brains of a duck are smaller than those of a ducks' rights activist but not by much. The noticeable structures of a duck brain are the cerebellum, the cerebral hemispheres, and the optic lobes. The cerebellum controls balance and acts as the autopilot during flight. The pair of hemispheres function as a computer center that stores and analyzes sensory information. The optic lobes not only analyze all visual readings, they also link the data with flight muscles engaged to avoid ground artillery.

BODY

Before ducks reach Big Babe Lake, their bodies are covered with feathers. Duck feathers have the same chemical composition as scales and are thought to document a lineage to reptiles. The long wide flight feathers and the body contour feathers are made up of thousands of spines called barbules. These spines separate as the feathers wear from use and are rezipped when ducks groom or "preen." During preening, an oil gland just above the tail is massaged to produce a fatty acid that is worked into and onto the feathers for waterproofing.

Feathers do wear out so most ducks shed their body feathers twice a year and wing feathers once. During these molts, males endure a bland "eclipse" plumage that makes them look like females, no small source of anxiety for rural ducks. Urban ducks, not so much. The colors of feathers come from chemical compounds or pigments that reflect or absorb a portion of the color spectrum that we can see. Melanin produces black, brown, and tans, carotenoid pigments produce yellow and red. Iridescent colors including most greens are the result of observing the changing angles of reflection on the rotating barbules of the feather.

BUCK'S HISTORICAL NOTE: There is a reason why puddle duck feathers are usually lighter than divers'. When the earth was being formed, early dabblers mistakenly sat on the hot water edges instead of the cooling floods and steamed the natural colors off their bottoms.

Duck feathers are attached to a skin that is best stripped and sautéed in bacon fat until crispy. The most important Chinese contribution to duck stuff was in the handling of such duck skin, where on hot days in a hot wok in hot oil in the capital city, duck skin is so separated from the muscle. Duck skin seems tighter on divers than on puddlers but then again, none of them seem to willingly give up their outer garments.

WINGS
Ducks originally landed vertically like a helicopter to protect their bottoms. The early wings would auto-rotate in their sockets and the flexing of the primary feathers would slow and finally cushion a controlled landing. More adventurous drakes would show off to the hens on the ground with dramatic fly-bys and touchdowns. Those that flew with their gear too close to the ground lost their ability to pass on their DNA but developed large vocal cords at the same time. Ducks with good hearing developed and passed on retractable gear.

LEGS AND FEET
The best swimmers have legs far back on the body and walk carefully to avoid falling forward. When ducks walk, most of the body weight is over the foot that's hitting the ground or the bird will lose its balance.

The three front toes are fused by a web that opens (with extended toes) when pushing water, folds (with bent toes) when moving forward. One of the few exceptions is the feet of the land-based Hawaiian goose, which are used to pick up loose change on resort hotel beaches.

Under the duck's wings, feathers, and skin covering is a complicated arrangement of hard and soft goods, including the soul, which is hard to identify in a small graphic.

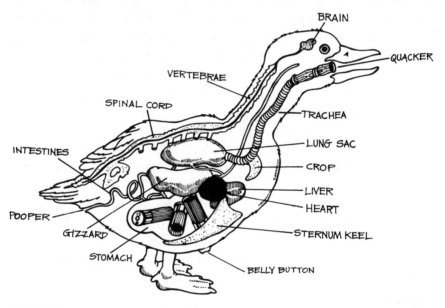

LUNGS

The lungs of a juvenile duck are pink and healthy. Adult bird lungs are typically clogged with secondary smoke from flying over urban centers; research shows that if the bird shortstops in a refuge, the damage is reversible.

GIZZARD

The gizzard is the food processor where nuts and seeds are ground for digestion and, according to researchers, lead pellets are ground for indigestion and the subsequent release of toxic oxides into the bloodstream. At the Poop and Go Blind Laboratory deep in the bowels of the U.S. Fish and Wildlife Service headquarters, scatologists force-feed lead pellets to imprisoned birds and have begun a new series of tests using steel shot without the shot cup. An unusual field discovery in Wisconsin has found surveyed ducks whose stomachs are full of whole shotgun shells accidentally ejected in the heat of the moment. Which only partially explains their low hunter success rate.

VENTRAL REGION

The duck butt contains all the parts normally associated with "down there." Thankfully, the sex organs are hidden from view. A drake's sexual equipment consists of testicles, which are attached inside, and an external "honker." The gonads vary in weight by season and are fully developed by spring. During the breeding season, the testes of a duck can weigh as much as one tenth of its total weight, much like a hunting buddy of Buck's during a night on the town. The pooper is the most active organ of the duck as the duck's intestinal system works overtime processing the food needed to fuel its high energy days.

CHAPTER 3

Duck Types

Ducks make up a large distinguished family in the wild kingdom. Technically, they are at the head of the class–Aves–which includes all birds. Ducks also belong to the smaller order–Anseriformes–that includes other game birds, geese, and swans. Only ducks belong to the family Anatidea—from the Latin word for "duck." The following are the American subfamilies or tribes that Buck's Dead Duck Society has brought so much grief.

> The ANATINI tribe of dabblers *(Anas)*: mallard and its regional variations, black duck, pintail, gadwall, widgeon, teal, and shoveler.
>
> The AYTHYINI tribe of inland divers, pochards, and scaups *(Aythya)*: canvasback, redhead, ring-necked duck, and lesser and greater scaup.
>
> The CAIRININI tribe of perching ducks *(Cairina)*: wood duck.
>
> The MERGINI tribe of sea ducks *(Bucephala)*: goldeneye, bufflehead, all merganser, eiders, scoters, old squaw, and harlequin.
>
> The OXYURINI tribe of stiff-tailed ducks *(Oxyura)*: ruddy duck.

When the tribal councils meet, they normally assemble as either dabbler or diver ducks.

Dabbling Ducks

In general, dabbling ducks tip up to eat plant parts in shallow water rather than dive. These puddle ducks spring directly into the air rather than run across the water to get airborne, fly higher with smaller groups (usually under a dozen birds), and drift down on larger wings with more colorful speculums than diving ducks.

Diving Ducks

The diving ducks, either the freshwater or bay ducks of the tribe Aythyini or the old salts from the seaduck tribe Mergini, dive deep to eat and escape danger. The bay ducks–canvasbacks, redheads, ring-necks, and greater and lesser scaups—are most like dabbling ducks; the sea ducks—scooters, eiders, harlequins, oldsquaws, goldeneyes, buffleheads, and mergansers—look and act much differently in their coastal saltwater environment.

The Swedish botanist Carolus Linnaeus systematized the scientific names of all waterfowl with two Latin names. The first name, the genus, is capitalized. The second name, the species, follows in small letters. Often the species name came as a reward for good service. Famous naturalists were infamous for flattering a scientist rather than anteing up a bonus from expedition coffers. Buck accepts the wordsmithing of the American Ornithologists Union, yet in his inimitable fashion makes classification even easier to understand by putting the words from dead languages into sportsman's English. Buck has at least one popular nickname for each game bird, a tag that identifies common individual physical characteristics such as red legs or bull necks. Nicknames do vary from blind to blind but Buck-sters everywhere agree that any drake that flies in range of Buck's blind on Big Babe Lake is a darn fool.

WATERFOWL IDENTIFICATION

There are two ways to identify ducks: at a distance or up close. Silhouette, sound, individual and flock flight characteristics, colors, and knowledge of typical habitat are the cross-references of a hunter's first notice. Up close, the choices are to use key features of the genus, then species. Traditional identification is becoming more difficult to master with savvy wild ducks switching habitats, changing flyways, and varying flight patterns to confuse the ordinary duck hunter. Resident shooters have even noted drake mallards rolling in dirt to disguise their bright colors before flying over Buck's blind.

As a public service, Buck has convinced Babe Peterson, head bartender and director of happy-hour etiquette, to share her species identification program as developed leaning on the railing outside the Valhalla Lounge.

Her system is accurate, even in the early part of the season when some drakes may still be in eclipse plumage, and is usually based on the tail feathers, attached if shot by Buck or not if shot at by nonresidents. Babe wants all Bucksters to know that if she hasn't seen all the species with her own eyes, it isn't because she didn't want to. Not all ducks can be hunted in all states, but that doesn't mean Buck hasn't hunted all of them, given the state of mind he's in.

BLACK DUCK, AMERICAN, *Anas rubripes* (redfooted duck)

Nicknames: Black or Dusky Mallard

BABE'S ID: The *canard noir* looks like a big sooty hen mallard. Both sexes have white borders on a purple speculum. Historically important to the East Coast gunner, these shy loners have suffered from habitat loss, lead poisoning, and overgunning. Given a choice, a female black duck prefers the stud services of a drake mallard, which explains why black duck drakes prefer quiet isolated pools and ponds far from the game farm mallard morons that threaten family integrity. In the uneasy truce, black ducks will fly with mallards but try to persuade the empty green heads to fly point.

BLACK DUCK

BUFFLEHEAD, *Bucephala albeola* (white bullhead)

Nickname: Buffalo-head

BABE'S ID: Big white triangle patch behind the eye on a purple-black drake head. During courtship, a drake's crest may become erect, which is a real lady-killer. Buffleheads nest in small tree cavities in temperate forests but not so small a cavity as to crack eggs already in the carton.

BUFFLEHEAD

   This bird is named for its oversized buffalo-shaped head on the smallest diving body. If retired market hunters knew there was a remnant population of buffalo-heads, this little butterball would be in a heap of big trouble. Also called helldiver for its habit of flying low and fast and, once on the water, diving quickly from danger.

CANVASBACK, *Aythya valisineria*

Nickname: Bullneck

BABE'S ID: Exhibits more white in flight than any other duck and is the only pochard with a two-inch culmen. It's reported that when Jack London lived in San Francisco, his rule was to eat a raw duck every day and that duck had to be a canvasback, which is another reason why he's not alive today—those two-inch culmens are killers. A wedge head is distinguished by a straight line from the top of its head to the tip of its beak, unlike the redhead, which has a nasal profile more like a ski jump. Canvasback nests are appropriated by the smaller redheads and an occasional bold ruddy duck, which qualifies them to be the queens rather than the kings of ducks and is a good reason to expand the season.

   This waterbird's favorite food is the commonly misspelled wild celery, *Vallisneria*, hence the bird's Latin name. The plant was named after an Italian naturalist of the seventeenth century who couldn't spell that good either.

CANVASBACK

COOT, AMERICAN, *Fulica americana*

Nicknames: Mud or Marsh Hen; Black Duck (Wisconsin)

BABE'S ID: Gray overall with gray-and-white bill. A member of the rail family, the coot's breeding display reveals the white undertail feathers, which, like the white jockey shorts of a construction worker, drives coot hens nuts. A coot head characteristically bobs while the body is walking or swimming; all this movement is part and parcel of this demonstrative bird's life. Being small and ugly, coots spend much of their time defending their "space" and fighting real and imagined enemies. Buck's backdoor neighbor used to swear by the breast meat of the coot. Among other things.

COOT

Eli Haydel describes the coot as a flying Studebaker because in silhouette, the front can't be distinguished from the back, except by the direction of flight.

OLD COOT

COOT, OLD, *Fulica seniorana* (retired coot)

Nickname: Snowbird (Florida, Arizona)

BABE'S ID: Gray where feathered, wrinkled else-where. The symbolic tribal duck of a small band of Native-like Americans called the Twingnuts living along the southern shores of Washington State. Led by the great Chief Toke-Em-If-You-Got-Em, the Twingnuts are petitioning the Great White Father for legal tribal recognition so they can buy used-but-looks-new casino equipment from the great white warrior Chief Trump of the Atlantic City tribe. A distant cousin of the mis-chievous raven, the old coot provides the tribe with gifts appropriated from nearby trailer parks. During the banned Line Dance of the Brown Spirit Waters, the ceremonial mask of the old coot is worn by the Buckster, another old coot warrior from the tribe of Goth.

CORMORANT, DOUBLE CRESTED,
Phalacrocorax auritus (eared cormorant)

Nicknames: Shag, Double Crested Mallard (Wisconsin)

BABE'S ID: A large fish-eater perched in a tree, with wings out-stretched to dry. The cormorant is not a real duck but it's one of the first waterfowl that juveniles or nonresidents shoot. The shied-poke pays the

CORMORANT

price of being in the wrong place at the wrong time but since these fish-mongers eat their weight in fins each day, it's about time they were taught a lesson in conservation.

DUCK, DAFFY, *Cinemas cartoonicus*
Nickname: Dethpicable Duck
BABE'S ID: Armlike wings and a white stripe around its neck like an emaciated brant. Self-described through a lisping quack as "Me? I'm just a crazy darn fool duck." Hunted by Porky Pig and later Elmer Fudd, this short, round-bottomed game bird was revealed to be unfairly wearing a bullet-proof vest under his contour feathers. This daffy duck short-stopped in 1942 to "see what this winter business is all about" and hasn't been seen aloft on the flyways since. Available on the airwaves only.

Daffy was first identified by famed celluloid naturalists the Warner Brothers in 1937.

DUCK, DONALD, *Amusementicus disneyyas*
Nickname: Carny rat
BABE'S ID: A little avian Fauntleroy stuffed in a joy-boy sailor outfit. This fat, domesticated drake is largely responsible for decoying unsuspecting vacationers into a pricey fiefdom that contains none of the true magic of the natural kingdom. First sighted in 1934 as a foil to a mousy-looking pessimist, this aging, nonmigratory star of screen and strip has

had a long history of irascibility. Off the record, even his old girlfriend thinks he deserves an open season.

DUCK, SITTING, *Georges armedweak custerissima* (dead duck)

Nickname: Curly

BABE'S ID: Yellow feathers on robust, yet stupid body. A pioneer drake known for its preening ego and political ambition. On an armed migration along the Mississippi Flyway, this nest-robbing militarist tangled with a wronged resident flock led by the genius of the genus, Tatanka Iyotake, and got seriously impaled on the not-so-little Big Horn of the white man's dilemma, and that's no bull.

COMMON EIDER

EIDER, COMMON, *Somateria mollissima* (very soft body wool)

Nickname: Shoal Duck

BABE'S ID: White back, black cap. The largest duck of the Northern Hemisphere rafts up at night far offshore. Foraging just beyond the surf, these five-pounders will go sixty feet for a common blue mussel. In Iceland, eggers pluck down and eggs from the nests of the eider colonies. Offshore Norwegian islanders have cultivated eiders longer but still you can't buy a good-looking Volvo sedan, even with a lot down.

The **KING EIDER,** *Somateria spectabilis* (showy body wool), is a very deep diving duck with a reputation of going down over one hundred feet for a starfish. The queen eider does not have the regal bump on her head and, without the full protection of the court, is often treated as a commoner.

The **SPECTACLED EIDER,** *Somateria fischeri* (showy body by Fischer), seems to be wearing spectacles or eyeglasses. If the spectacles of the older eider came in different focal lengths, the bird wouldn't be on the threatened list.

The **STELLER'S EIDER,** *Polysticta stelleri* (many-spotted stellar), is named for the naturalist who suffered from German measles on Bering's expedition to the Arctic. This very wild eider is also called the soldier or, in season, dead duck, for its habit of swimming single file along the less accessible coast of Alaska.

FULVOUS WHISTLING DUCK, *Dendrocygna bicolor* (two-colored tree swan)

Nickname: Large Whistling Teal

BABE'S ID: Black eye patch on a shiny white head. The hens and drakes of the widest-spread species of whistling duck in North America not only look alike but also sound alike, which makes neither feel secure. The only other whistling duck seen in the states is the black-bellied whistling duck, which prefers making love standing on dry land, a social custom common all over south Texas and, for that matter, east, west, and north Texas, too. Also Louisiana and parts of Florida.

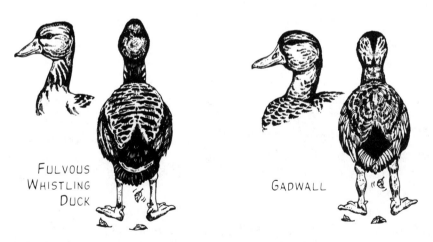

FULVOUS WHISTLING DUCK

GADWALL

GADWALL, *Anas strepera* (obstreperous anas)

Nickname: Poacher

BABE'S ID: Only puddle duck with white in its speculum. The gadwall was originally thought to be a trash duck but its freshwater diet is almost all vegetative matter. This gray duck is one of the few dabblers that dives and has the unenvied reputation of poaching other ducks' food. Shame!

From their habit of swinging back for a second look at decoys, gadwalls are a favorite of nonresident shooters.

COMMON GOLDENEYE

GOLDENEYE, COMMON, *Bucephala clangula* (noisy bullhead)

Nickname: Whistler

BABE'S ID: Only large male diver with a mostly white body and a yellow eye in a greenish black head with a small white patch between the eye and bill. Very independent and restless, goldeneyes don't respond to calls or stool well. When alarmed, they lie low in the water and dive deep at just the flash of a gun. Goldeneyes have the most complex and aggressive social displays including a female neck-dip and light screech that is shameless.

The nickname comes from the whistle sound made from the narrowed web on the drake's last two primaries. These tree ducks are called *Gogol* in Russian; when Buck calls them in his adopted tongue, they are Dead Souls.

GOLDENEYE, BARROW'S, *Bucephala islandica* (Icelandic bullhead)

Nickname: Whistler

BABE'S ID: This flat-headed little drake diver has crescent-shaped white cheek markings and a glossy purple head on a blacker body with a pattern of oval white spots on the scapulars. The common and the

Barrow's goldeneye nest in tree cavities in temperate climates and, in those close quarters, who's keeping an eye on whom?

This duck was named in honor of Sir John Barrow, yet another Secretary of British Admiralty who feathered his nest in any cavity that was available.

HARLEQUIN DUCK, *Histrionicus histrionicus* (of the theater or stage)

Nickname: Painted Duck

BABE'S ID: A slate blue duck with white stripes or spots. Even with all their bright markings, Sam Blake says they are like smoke: one minute you see them, the next you can't. Our only torrent duck does not migrate far but does fly inland to nest. This buoyant whitewater rafter forages fast mountain rapids and coastal heavy surfs for animal matter and is avoided by gourmands who prefer to chew the crustaceans and mollusks first.

HARLEQUIN DUCK

In the theater, appearance is everything, and speed is appreciated when trying to ditch the critics. So this bird is aptly named after Harlequin, the clown of Italian comic opera.

LABRADOR DUCK, *Anus extinctus*

Nickname: Sand-Shoaled Duck

BABE'S ID: Unlikely. John James Audubon called it the Pied Duck but he couldn't find the nesting sites either and had to paint them from

LABRADOR DUCK

a hunter's sample. This extinct mussel-feeding duck may have lost its fragile food source or it could have been eaten by a Labrador from Newfoundland. The last known sighting in 1875 and the last known specimen shot in 1878 were both on Long Island, which is now the home of a much less distinguished commercial duck.

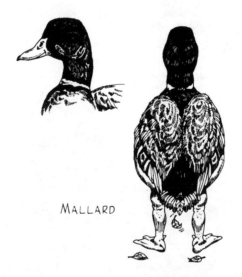

MALLARD

MALLARD, *Anas platyrhynchos* (broadbill duck)

Nickname: Greenhead

BABE'S ID: There seem to be two types of male mallards, a less bright resident or early migrant and a puffy-headed late migrant marked by red legs. The mallard hens look like gadwalls with an iridescent blue wing speculum and always quack when flushed. The drakes are very aggressive and have fathered countless illegitimate black duck ducklings. The reckless sexual predation of the drake greenhead threatens to genetically swamp the gene pools of the mottled duck and others. Drakes of the smaller island races of mallards look more like hens, which is probably a good thing in those landlocked matriarchal societies.

When Buck shoots, drakes explode midair, defying identification. The other half of the pair must be a hen. It seems mallards have been around forever. Greenheads from the Pleistocene period have been found in the Rancho La Brea Tar Pits in Los Angeles, the first California development entirely underwritten by the Asphalt Foundation. Duckinmallard to Lewis and Clark, the common mallard was easily domesticated by the Chinese some two thousand years ago. Now fat mallard eunuchs even tease hunters by walking through hotel lobbies. It's not clear in the hotel literature if there is a season on these domesticated dolts but it's likely the morons know how to quack for hotel security if they see a camouflage jacket or retriever nearby.

HOODED MERGANSER

MERGANSER, HOODED, *Mergus cucullatus*
(hooded diver goose)

Nickname: Ah'@#%&*! or, in mixed company, Fuzzy Head

BABE'S ID: Relatively long dark tail on a long dark skinny body topped with a long skinny bill. This quiet freshwater duck nests in hollows or cavities in dead trees along the south end of Big Babe Lake where Buck has a special blind built for visually impaired nonresident shooters with a preference for a fish duck indigenous to North America.

MERGANSER, COMMON, *Mergus merganser*
(diver goose diver)

Nickname: Ah'@#%&*! or, in polite company, Goosander
BABE'S ID: Pure white or pinkish-colored breast. Another shied-poke.

MERGANSER, RED-BREASTED, *Mergus serrator*
(sawer diver)

Nickname: Ah'@#%&*! or, in polite company, Fish Duck
BABE'S ID: Drake in nuptial plumage has a green head, shaggy double crest, and white ascot. This saltwater fisherman has a wider and more northern participation in nonresident game bags.

MOTTLED DUCK

MOTTLED DUCK, *Anas fulvigula* (reddish-yellow throat)

Nickname: Florida, Texas, or Summer Mallard
BABE'S ID: A small, not-so-dark black duck with a buff throat. The mottled duck spends its life along the Gulf Coast, randomly migrating east and west to keep one giant step ahead of the great horned feral greenhead.

OLDSQUAW, *Clangula hyemalis* (wintry noise)

Nickname: Long-Tailed Duck
BABE'S ID: Elongated tail and long, white scapulars of the male. The drake call was described by the late Norm Strung as falling between the moo of a cow and the grunt of a goose. The most arctic of the family with no fear of shotguns, oldsquaws fly fast and close to surface, zigging and

zagging, twisting and turning, and, unlike other sea ducks, often splashing down to dive up to a hundred feet using wings that blast the guided missile back out of water and out of range.

OLDSQUAW

The oldsquaw was named by Cree Indian patriarchs who ascribed similarities to an old Cree woman's incessant chatter. This is unfortunate because drake oldsquaws are the real loudmouths, which gives you an idea how feminism is doing among the Cree.

PEKIN DUCK, *Anas restauranta chinesa*

Nickname: Dinner

BABE'S ID: The most popular domestic duck, a large white mutant mallard imported from China in late 1800s. By adding the letter G, a

PEKING DUCK

waterfowler has **PEKING DUCK**, a large crispy-skinned duck found on all major fryways. No license is required, but a twenty-four-hour notice is recommended.

PINTAIL, *Anas acuta* (sharptail duck)

Nickname: Sprig

BABE'S ID: Dark brown head with a long craning neck and long tail. These wary, elegantly colored birds have had the greatest population decline in the past thirty years and anyone who takes more than their share is a **PINHEAD**, a subspecies of *Anus anus*.

PINTAIL

The pintail is often called the "Greyhound of the air," more for the ability to take many stops on a long journey than an ability to take on passengers.

PUDDLE-DUCK, JEMIMA, *Beatrix pottercus* (English muddled duck)

Nickname: Goosey Duck

BABE'S ID: White body and a snappy DKNY kerchief. A literary duck that looks more like a goose and, in her misadventures, acts as dumb as a goose. This hen is so anxious to hatch her eggs that she is taken in by a smooth-talking, predator with sandy-colored whiskers.

Kep the retriever collie and two foxhound puppies finally rescue the little lady but it is too close a call.

PUDDLE-DUCK

Save the puddle-duck! Buy sandy-colored whiskered fur!

REDHEAD, *Aythya americana* (American waterbird)

Nickname: Fiddler Duck

BABE'S ID: Shorter, more rounded head than canvasback, bluish bill with white ring. The redhead is half a pound lighter and eats less animal matter than its big brother, the canvasback. If Jack London had lived only on redheads, his domestic life would have been much simpler.

REDHEAD

REDNECK DUCK, *Anuscephala masondixona* (borderline butthead)

Nickname: Hey You

BABE'S ID: Soiled blue collar. A heavy-lidded, slow-witted, happy-hour bully with clumsy, messy, and noisy courtship displays. Incapable of pair-forming, which is a good thing when you think of the gene pool he's been swimming in.

REDNECK DUCK

RING-NECKED DUCK, *Aythya collaris* (collared waterbird)

Nickname: Ringbill

BABE'S ID: Dark wings with pearly gray speculum and pale gray to bright white band around the bill. A pochard named for the faint brown or chestnut ring around its collar at the base of the drake's neck. The cleric's collar qualifies the drake for the name *priest duck*, but his hen would have nun of that.

RING-NECKED

RUDDY DUCK, *Oxyura jamaicensis* (sharp-tailed duck)

Nickname: Butterball

BABE'S ID: The male's oversized head with snow white cheeks, powder blue bill, and dark crown. Originally discovered in Jamaica, the ruddy is named for its ruddy complexion and is the only member of the spiked or stiff-tailed duck tribe most American hunters will see. The odd squat-bodied little duck with tail feathers extending beyond the coverts is also the only American duck with an inflatable air sac off its windpipe. During courtship, the drake slaps its bill against the inflated tracheal area and breast, producing bubbling and belching love sounds, much like the sounds of Buck's buddies at last call. The spiketail swims with its tail erect

RUDDY DUCK

like a bathroom toy and, in Buck's experience, prefers the quiet company of decoys. If absolutely necessary, the ruddy will take the time necessary to get its fat little body up off the water and then and only then is it a flight duck. Buck won't shoot a ruddy duck. With its reverse molt, it is too much like a songbird. The ruddy crash-lands in the water by itself; true waterfowlers can dry-fire and count imaginary coup.

SCAUP, GREATER, *Aythya marila* (charcoal waterbird)

Nickname: Bluebill

BABE'S ID: A greenish head and a long broad white stripe across both primary and secondary wing feathers. The greater scaup nests in the Arctic and sub-Arctic, rafts on big-water lakes and seas, and—with decoys—is easily tolled for thee.

SCAUP

The name *scaup* may have come from the British word for mussel beds, or the sound made by a hen, or from a favorite cheese potato dish served at midwestern potlucks.

SCAUP, LESSER, *Aythya affinis* (related waterbird)

Nickname: Little Bluebill

BABE'S ID: Purple head and white speculum. The lesser scaup is more an inland bird and winters on coasts. Buck shot his first double on two crossing lessers and didn't think lesser of them for their mistake.

SCOTER, BLACK, *Melanitta nigra* (black duck)

Nickname: Sea Coot

BABE'S ID: All black, except yellow knot at base of bill. This blue mussel and razor clam eater breeds primarily in Alaska.

SURF SCOTER

SCOTER, SURF, *Melanitta perspicillata* (conspicuous duck)

Nickname: Skunkhead
BABE'S ID: The male has a skunklike white forehead, nape patches, and a handy black bull's-eye on the sides of its beak.

SCOTER, WHITE-WINGED, *Melanitta fusca* (dark duck)

Nickname: Bullcoot
BABE'S ID: The male has white secondaries and a teardrop white eye patch. The largest, showiest, and most abundant sea scoter likes the same shellfish as man, but then again young scoters can't locate the gun sounds of the more evolved shellfish-eaters in the blind.

SEADUCK, JONATHAN LIVINGONCE, *Anas cannabis* (doper duck)

Nickname: Smokey
BABE'S ID: Nondescript carrion-eating seabird. A relic population of free-thinking California beach birds first recorded in the early seventies. Once thought to be the image of the Divine Duck, this offbeat subspecies known for its high-altitude, high-attitude aerobatics is now rarely spotted along any major flyway. The call melody of this sea duck resembles a minor unrelated Bach fugue, in the key of G-whiz.

SHOVELER, *Anas clypeata* (duck with a shield)

Nickname: Spoonbill
BABE'S ID: Tail feathers that do not include the curled upper tail coverts of the mallard. From their reputation of being easy decoys, some shooters say shovelers aren't too bright but some shovelers fly directly to

SHOVELER

Hawaii, which is more than many duck hunters do. If it looks sorta like a mallard, flies sorta like a mallard, but doesn't quack like a mallard, it's the state mallard of Wisconsin.

The Twingnuts of southwest Washington call the shoveler "Yuk-Gut-Duk" for the intestines that reach up to ten feet long.

TEAL, BLUE-WINGED, *Anas discors* (discord-causing duck)

Nickname: Blue-winged Devils

BABE'S ID: A formation of six birds, the flying elite of the feathered air corps. The male in full nuptial plumage has a plum-colored head with a crescent-shaped white patch on each cheek. Both sexes have a green speculum to throw off the ground observers and the blue-winged hen is very similar in appearance to the cinnamon teal hen. The only unat-

BLUE-WINGED TEAL

tached hens are hooked at tail feather conventions by drakes making improper sexual overflights. Blue-winged teal are unusually sensitive to the cold and leave the breeding grounds of Minnesota and Wisconsin early on a long migration to their winter home base.

These seed-eating, shallow-water birds are Buck's favorite duck. Dorothy's, too.

TEAL, CINNAMON, *Anas cyanoptera* (dark blue-winged duck)

Nickname: Blue-winged Teal

BABE'S ID: Blurry red fuselage, cobalt blue coverts, green speculum. The eyes of a young drake turn cinnamon at a couple months old. Another early migrant, this teal jets south in pairs or small family groups from as far north as the sub-Arctic to get even more red-breasted on the patios of their winter homes in Mexico.

CINNAMON TEAL

TEAL, GREEN-WINGED, *Anas crecca* (duck that sounds)

Nickname: Redhead

BABE'S ID: Light gray back, green speculum, and green eye shadow. The green-winged is the smallest duck in North America and flies over fifty miles an hour, faster than the other two teal. *Don't tell the Blue-winged Devils!* The green-wingeds also have a reputation for being even wilder than the Blue-winged Devils, proving military discipline has a price.

GREEN-WING TEAL

WIDGEON, AMERICAN, *Anas americana*

Nickname: Baldpate

BABE'S ID: White upper wing coverts on both sexes. The drake has a gray-brown head with dark green eye shadow and a white crown. The widgeon eats stems and leaves of plants and steals food from coots and redheads. A baldpate fed on widgeon grass is very wary but, once in range or coming out of the range, very easy to put down.

AMERICAN WIDGEON

Baldpate is a sexist term for the pale white head feathers atop the drake's head. At least a bald-pated drake looks distinguished. A bald-pated hen just looks bald-headed.

WIDGEON, EUROPEAN, *Anas penelope*

Nickname: Eurasian or Redhead Widgeon

BABE'S ID: The aristocratic foreigner has a yellow baldpate. Occasionally seen on the East Coast, rarely on the West Coast. The Latin name for this duck is the same as the wife of Odysseus, who waited faithfully for his return from the Trojan War.

If a waterfowler thinks his Penelope will wait faithfully for his return from pursuing this redhead, he hasn't been watching Oprah. There may be some connection, then again, maybe not.

WOOD DUCK, *Aix sponsa* (betrothed waterfowl)

Nickname: Woodie

BABE'S ID: Noggin and neck shiny with glossy green and purple. Both sexes fly like miniature Concordes with their heads high and beaks down. Member of a subfamily of perching ducks that have sharp clawed feet and powerful back toes to climb in and out of the tree nest. Wood ducks were not always plentiful. In a shameful chapter in our sporting past, fly fishermen used punt guns to remove wood duck feathers for tying Light and Dark Cahills and Quill Gordon flies. In 1918, feds finally closed the sea-

WOOD DUCK

son on wood ducks but at the same time should have also required fly fishermen to use artificial plugs. They still should. It wasn't until 1941 that American fly tiers figured out a way to dye mallard feathers; a few states tossed a wood duck into the game bag to replace the mallards fly fishermen were false-casting to.

AND A LITTLE GOOSE ON THE SIDE

BARNACLE GOOSE, *Branta leucopis* (white face)

Nickname: None

BABE'S ID: Predominately white head and light gray upper wing. Medieval scholars believed this goose was born from a goose barnacle, which explains why the medievalists are where they are—dead! Based on this belief, however, big Church fathers did bless the barnacle goose as seafood, making it okay to eat on Fridays, which made the other goose families turn Protestant.

BRANT GOOSE, *Branta bernicla* **(Atlantic or common brant)**

Nickname: Brant

BABE'S ID: Black except for five to six prominent white slashes on throat. This small sea goose loves the exposed eelgrass of shallow bays and estuaries on low or slack tides. Old-timers used to look at the rectum of a brant to judge its table-worthiness; if they've been eating sea lettuce, the brant rectum turns greenish and the bird should go to a neighbor. Old-timers can be such butts for neighbors.

BRANT

BLACK BRANT, *Branta bernicla nigricans (black brant)*

Nickname: Pacific Brant

BABE'S ID: Whitish upper flanks and more extensive white patches on neck. This five-pounder has one of the longest migrations of any waterfowl species, up to three thousand miles from northern Alaska, flying nonstop and largely out of range to Baja. Harvest this goose before it loses its baby fat.

CANADA GOOSE, *Branta canadensis* **(Canada bird)**

Nickname: Honker

BABE'S ID: Long black neck with clear white cheek patches attached to a big gray-brown body. Buck counts at least ten separate races or subspecies that need harvesting and divides all honkers into large or small and migrating or resident populations. If they are large and migrating or large and resident, they should be harvested as soon as possible. If they are small and migrate along the West Coast, they, too, should be harvested but pay close attention: There are a few protected birds on that flyway. Small honkers should be harvested if for no other reason than to get a clearer shot at the larger ones.

EMPEROR GOOSE, *Anser canagicus* (goose of Kanaga Island/Alaskan Aleutian Islands)

Nickname: Eskimo Goose

BABE'S ID: Dark gray goose with white head and neck. Rarely seen out of Alaska, those that breed on the ex-Soviet side of the Bering Sea hope the new Moscow maximas will release the **EMPRESS GOOSE**, *Anser tsarinas*, from the goose gulags of Siberia.

HAWAIIAN GOOSE, *Branta sandvicensis*

Nicknames: Mountain Goose, Nene Goose

BABE'S ID: The sides of the head and neck are buff-colored with distinctive black lines. The state bird of Hawaii is found only on the islands of Hawaii and Maui. Although protected from hunting, the state and two units of the National Park System raise captive birds to feed U.S. congressmen on winter vacation.

ROSS GOOSE, *Anser rossii*

Nickname: Warty-Nosed Goose

BABE'S ID: A small snow goose with warty protuberances. Breeding just above the Arctic Circle, the quiet Ross goose parts company with other species at the border of Montana and heads southwest to central California for the winter. It's only when they ditch the unsuspecting white goose crowd heading for the big guns of the delta that the Ross goose, without the snow's grinning patches, cracks a smile.

This goose is named after a Mr. Ross, a chief of the Hudson's Bay Company who probably had warty protuberances where his nose met his face.

SNOW GOOSE, LESSER, *Anser caerulescens caerulescens* (blue, blue goose)

Nicknames: Snow, Snow Goose

BABE'S ID: A blue-phase lesser has a blue body and white head. The dark gene is dominant so this is not just a phase the young go through. The explosive growth of this bird population contains great risk and until the Pope agrees on avian birth control, the lessers may not be delivered from plague, pestilence, and famine. Widely distributed across the Arctic, many of these birds are ex-Soviet émigrés. While most adult birds return to the traditional homeland off Siberia, the less wary young are attracted to the looser lifestyle of the Alaskans, especially the loose-as-a-goose lifestyle of Buck's duck hunting pal down on Turnagain Spit.

SNOW GOOSE, GREATER, *Anser caerulescens atlantica*

Nickname: Atlantic Blue Goose

BABE'S ID: If you see what looks like a white greater snow goose over Big Babe Lake, stay put. The winds from the east can't get worse. If you see what looks to be a blue-phase greater snow goose, the strong winds from the east can't get colder.

WHITE-FRONTED GOOSE, *Anser albifrons*
(white-foreheaded goose)

Nicknames: Specklebelly, Prairie Brant

BABE'S ID: White facial markings surround the bill of the adult bird, with brown coloring on the body and a white butt. These five-pounders are the most widely distributed geese in the world. Known in Europe as the laughing goose, one white-fronted was reported to have lived over forty-five years, and if that bird is in your game bag, the last laugh is on you.

WILD SWANS

Ed Zern, the late great outdoor humorist, in his book *To Hell with Hunting* summed up all the swan stuff a casual observer may need: "Tame swans live in parks, and hiss at people. Wild swans are swans that do not have a park to hiss in."

MUTE SWAN, *Cygnus olor* (swan swan)

Nickname: Swan

BABE'S ID: The only white swan to have a reddish orange bill with an enlarged black knob at the base. Originally imported from Europe to be released as a park bird, Tchaikovsky wrote a ballet about this bird and its refuge in the Midwest. No season yet. A major source of mortality is overhead wires, a subject the power company's spokeswan is mute on.

TRUMPETER SWAN, *Cygnus buccinator* (trumpeter swan)

Nickname: Swan

BABE'S ID: A swan with no yellow patch on its bill. This is the largest waterfowl in North America and can weigh more than forty teal. The bird is so heavy that some swans homestead and give up their migrating ways. No season yet. A major source of mortality is unsuccessful airborne mating with ultralights.

TUNDRA SWAN, *Cygnus columbianus*

Nickname: Whistling Swan

BABE'S ID: A half-pint trumpeter with a small yellow patch in front of its eye. The healthy population splits east and west and those hunting these fifteen-pound sky carp should wear protective helmets.

Lewis and Clark took the first specimen of this swan on the Columbia River. Not being well versed in the ways and means of catch-and-release, they didn't put it back

---

So Many Game Birds, So Little Time

The marshes are full of game birds so deep

That I must blast before I sleep

That I must blast before I sleep.

— R. Frosted Flake

CHAPTER 4

THE LIFE OF A DUCK

Do ducks actually have one life to live or are they just feathered containers of behavior patterns? Are ducks little people? Anthropomorphism has been profitable for theme park operators, but at a real price to a mature understanding of nature. On the other hand, mechanomorphism fails to appreciate the role of senses in an intense presence. To answer these and many other important questions, Buck's research teams have carefully studied wild ducks in captivity and documented a complicated set of behavior patterns.

A DAY IN THE LIFE OF A DUCK

Morning: Walking around, quacking, picking at each other.

Afternoon: Walking around, quacking, picking at each other.

Evening: Walking around, quacking, picking at each other.

The daily activity is changed and complete when food and water are included:

Morning: Walking around, drinking, quacking, eating, picking at each other.

Afternoon: Same.

Evening: Same.

If the full daily activity is multiplied by 365 with a little time set aside for going potty, you would end up with a year in the life of a duck.

When does the life of a duck actually begin? Biologists say life begins at conception. Sex therapists say lively conception is life itself. Mother Superior says you don't need to know any of the physical stuff until you are a pair and maybe not even then. Behaviorists say life starts on the first day. Calendar publishers say life begins on January 1. Romantic that he is, Buck says the life of a duck starts as a good thought first given expression during courtship.

COURTSHIP
The cast of characters in duck courtship rituals may include one male with one female (monogamy) or one male with two or more females (polygyny). Polygyny is common to the shameless mallard, which has slept with over forty other species, qualifying the greenhead for associate membership in the Dead Duck Society. Other variations include one female with two or more males (polyandry), or a combined effort at both polygyny and polyandry (polygamy). If you think these ritual pairings are confusing, think of how it must be for the bird-brained participants.

HOW ARE MATES SELECTED?
First of all, males usually outnumber females on the wintering grounds and intense competition means few juvenile males get a date. All hens do. Females are the selectors in most courtships and predictably incite males to make fools out of themselves. A hen mallard will call in a unusually seductive voice. An interested male quickly responds by shaking its head, dipping its bill into water, flashing the secondary iridescent feathers, or rising up in the water to show its stuff. Seaduck hen displays are even more elaborate. The Barrow's goldeneye hen incites the male by moving its head from side to side while stretching its neck, which drives the male quackers. Pintail and lesser scaup hens encourage aerial pursuit; these chases are intended to be courtship but often turn into attempted rapes, putting an entirely different spin on the flight pattern.

WHAT DO HENS REALLY WANT IN A MATE?
Do they want a mate that looks like their father? No, they quack, hens want a mate that has any or all of the following attributes:

PROPERTY OWNER: A drake with an established territory provides a safe place to eat and nest.

PHYSICALLY FIT: A drake in fine fettle is able to defend the home and hearth against all challengers and, as a special bonus, has fewer parasites.

GOOD-LOOKING: A drake that looks good, with groomed, brightly colored feathers, intimidates other males and makes other hens jealous.

A NICE BUTT: A drake with a well-defined ventral region is the preferred companion for the annual end-of-migration reunions and other *Anas* family gatherings.

MATURE: An experienced drake is more sensitive to the needs of a modern hen, remembers important holidays, and is secure enough in his own skins, so to speak, to let the hen spread her wings, so to speak again.

A GOOD SENSE OF HUMOR: A drake that has flown over nonresident shooters will appreciate all the foibles of just being a duck.

The actual courtship of a duck is composed of a series of rituals that stimulate and synchronize the sexual rhythms of the other sex and ensure sexual and species specificity. Each species of duck has its own set of rituals and the form of these rituals or "displays" varies by function: pair-forming, pair-maintaining, and displays for the facilitation of copulation. Pair-forming displays are more deliberate and elaborate than those that maintain the relationship or signal copulation, which is understandable to anyone who has been married for a while.

Primary pair-forming courtship occurs at the end of the fall migration. Most dabbling ducks, such as mallards, are paired up before heading north in the spring. Some ducks, like gadwalls, start looking for partners early and fly south in pairs. Many of the freshwater divers are couples by the time they are halfway to the nesting grounds and almost all hens have a drake on their wing upon arrival. If the courtship is not completed on the wintering grounds, lovers quickly learn that the opportunities for making whoopee during a busy migration are limited: at the rest stops, hens are too tired to fool around, and courting a hen in formation disrupts the airflow patterns of the flight. However, high-concept fliers who are successful take great pride in their induction into the infamous Two Thousand Feet High Club.

Courtship among ducks has a proper sequence: falling in like, forming and maintaining a pair for appearance's sake, and then having wild and crazy duck sex. A drake greenhead advances quickly to step three. The proper pattern for other ducks may be altered if a brood did-n't hatch, was eaten by an animal, or was poached by a native. If the hen decides to try for a second nesting, she solicits a quickie from any male in the area. Normally, the sex life of a duck is more predictable.

COPULATION

When ducks make love or, as some spouses say, "do the Big Icky," bird biologists say they are "treading." Treading or copulation can occur as early as the fall. These early trysts are usually nonproductive and consid-ered practice by many, which really upsets Mother Church, which teaches that the act of pair-forming is sacred and only those who have pair-main-tained have the maturity to understand the responsibilities of sex and parenthood. Protestants, especially Lutherans, are a whole other story.

Only in a few species like the ostrich, duck, and goose is there an extraordinary erectile phallus inside the male vent. In Buck's scientific treatise *Drakes Are From Venus, Hens Wish They Had One* (Prescott, Wisconsin: Ate One Two Press, 1995), his research indicates that avian anatomical differences may have extraterrestrial origins. Any readers with an extra Jackson in their bill-folds who are willing to send it along can write for the grainy black-and-white pictures.

Once all the proper displays and calls have been made, duck sex begins with the drake approaching the hen from the rear and sliding up on the par-tially submerged lover, often grabbing or biting her by the back of the neck. In this position, the hen is unable to leave telltale wing scratches on the drake's back, which is Mother Nature's way of protecting what is laughingly called the duck family unit.

Prior to the actual act of treading, the tail of the hen moves aside and feathers turn to reveal the cloaca inside the vent, which houses, among other things, the female's "mountain of love."

The joining of two lovebirds lasts but a short moment but then again, they're only ducks. If a Buckster made that short a visit, he'd be drummed out of the Dead Duck Society unless, of course, the visited hen was a ducks' rights activist. Regardless of species, if the mating is not as exciting as it might be, treading becomes a treadmill and the relationship starts to tread water.

Postcopulatory activities vary by species. Typically, the male releases the nape of the hen's neck, makes a short call of triumph to the other drakes in the 'hood, and proudly swims off while the female bathes. Strong pairs call and rise together out of the water before bathing and swimming away. The little black scoter whistles a happy tune. The male ruddy duck politely faces his sexual partner, bubbles a thank-you, and rearranges his feathers before beating feet. Not one male duck of any species falls asleep after coitus, which is another good reason to blast these throwbacks.

If the treading is successful, the hen is pregnant and, in the biological sense, the life of a duck has truly begun.

BIRTH

Ducks begin their life in an egg. These eggs are stored in the egg carton of the pregnant mother duck until her contractions are less than one minute apart and her cloaca is properly dilated. A hen does not break water before she delivers; if enough hens did, there would be no such things as droughts. Once eggs start moving down the birth canal, the mother-to-be exhibits general nervousness since few male ducks take egg-laying classes with their hens and even fewer elect to stay near the delivery site.

First-time mothers (and all urban hens) quack with distress if the eggs are too big; call analysis indicates a resentment of the drake that put her in this condition. Old hens sleep through much of their delivery. The sight and touch of eggs activates the hen's pituitary gland to release a hormone called prolactin, stopping egg-laying and raising her temperature slightly. Incubation usually doesn't start until the last egg is laid and lasts from three to over five weeks. During incubation, brooding mothers line the nest of dead grass with their own feathers to warm and cushion the eggs. The eggs are then turned every so often so the embryos don't get stuck in the sunny-side-up position. With few exceptions, drakes get bored with this household routine and move on to begin their summer molt with the other guys out on big water.

How does a big duck know a small duck will come out of her egg? She doesn't! Even Daffy Duck has questioned, "Me . . . in an egg?" Grandparents-to-be can't tell if the eggs are the product of the hen and her mate; if there is a hint of marital discord, they anxiously await the hatch. In Denmark, ducks lay one ugly duckling egg in every clutch, which is suspicious until you remember how morally loose the Danes are. At least the color of duck eggs is predictable. They get their color from pigment cells in their ride down the oviducts and uterus.

Clutch size or number of ducklings depends on the species, the nesting environment, and the health of the bird. The ruddy duck hen will lay a dozen eggs in as many days. What's puzzling is that if all her eggs were gathered, they would weigh three times the one-pound mother. If a ruddy-faced human hen had offspring that weighed three times her weight, that would be the end of sex as Bucksters know it.

The eggs and the hen are most vulnerable while nesting. In remote areas of Canada and Alaska, natives living on subsistence have taken their toll on several now threatened species of geese. Environment Canada has decided that the best way to break the native population's reliance on goose eggs for breakfast is to substitute hash browns. The newly formed Prairie Pothole Potato Council hopes increased demand will sprout from their issuance of a set of free recipe cards featuring the tuber, printed in both French and Canadian English.

In the important American prairie pothole region, change in habitat has made nest predation even more significant. Predator controls on prairie wolves and then coyotes have opened dwindling habitat to the red fox, a mixed species that eats both the nesting hens and their eggs. There are estimates of a quarter-million red foxes in North Dakota alone. In the entire prairie pothole region, it's estimated that only one in ten nesting hens produces a brood and 70 percent of those losses are due to the egg-sucking fox, among other predators. For the population to remain stable, 15 percent of the broods must be successful. In the nesting areas around Big Babe Lake, Buck has solved the problem of furred egg suckers by placing Babe's pickled and peppered hard-boiled eggs in strategic predator spots. They weren't selling that good anyway.

A recent survey conducted by a conservation group found that a controlled nesting plot with predator species reduced to levels of the sixties had spring nest success rates of over 70 percent. Then again, everything was better in the sixties. The music, the food, the cars. Even in the fifties,

the duckling Baby Huey was able to compensate for his naiveté about the
true nature of the sandy-colored fox by his immense size and strength.

Buck's special duck conservation message:

BUY AND WEAR SANDY-COLORED FUR!

Once it's time for the egg to hatch, "pipping" occurs, taking a day or so.
The last egg to be laid is the last to hatch, yet the entire
clutch can be on their feet in five to six hours. Ducks
and geese are born with their eyes open and covered
with coats of natal down that would cost quite a
bit if they had to buy them from a major outfitter. Needing only a few hours to dry and fluff,
this light covering allows the little ones to
control their body temperature.

In what's called the prefledging period (from
a little over a month to two months for certain divers), much of the little
duck's time is spent playing little duck games such as Hide and Go Peep.
They have their own duck calls, which call manufacturers are shameless-
ly trying to imitate. The young learn by trial and error as they explore the
neighborhood. Harlequin ducklings practice riding the rapids. Young
eiders hold their noses and baby wood ducks open their eyes on their first
dives. Little greenheads try to tread water. On the water, an entirely new
group of predators appears: turtles, alligators, bass, and muskies take little
ones from below. Raptors cherry-pick the survivors from above.

In a perfect world, both parents would teach the kids how to act like
a duck but most duck dads have already taken off on a molt migration to
change clothes before heading south. Animal rights activists in the Fish
and Wildlife Service are organizing local chapters of "Hens Without
Drakes" and supporting legislation to force deadbeat dads into some form
of duckling support. Mom tries to hang in there as a single parent, but she
loses all her flight feathers when the kids are half grown and, tired and vulnerable to the sandy-colored fox, becomes more secretive as time goes by.

The siblings or "brood" generally stay together from hatching to the
first flight or "fledging." It is flight activity that establishes the relationship between waterfowl and the waterfowler.

CHAPTER 5

How Does a Duck Fly?

In any conversation about flight, the commonly asked question "How does a duck fly?" pales in comparison to the question "Why does a duck fly?" If there is no need for flight—chickens in corporate henhouses have no need to fly from natural predators—the development of a hard sternum is arrested and flightlessness occurs, which shows how good a deal Mother Nature cut the Colonel.

Ducks fly because if migrations were on walkways rather than flyways, early-morning and late-afternoon drive-time congestion would be unimaginable.

HOW DOES A DUCK FLY?

For a bird to fly, it needs big flight muscles, a high-energy metabolism, and, if available, a set of goggles and a white scarf. A bird is born to fly, much like a duck hunter is born to get wet. A bird's flight equipment can weigh up to 25 percent of its total weight even if its bones are hollow to reduce weight. The flight muscles are fibers full of oxygen-rich blood to fly hard and are conveniently located in the breast of the bird for easy handling in the kitchen.

Large outside breast muscles are attached to the underside of the upper arm bones for the more difficult task of pulling arms or wings down. An inner set of breast muscles is attached to the top side of the upper arm bones to pull the wings up. Both sets are attached to the breastbone. The deeper the breastbone, the more wing muscle the bird has. The stiffer the breastbone, the more likely the wing muscles have to be parboiled.

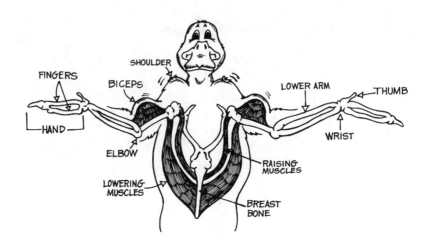

Flight feathers are attached to the wing bones. The primaries are attached to the hand and have the same freedom of movement. The shorter secondaries that provide flight support are attached to the lower bones. The tertiaries on the upper arm bone stabilize the bird. The arm bone's connected to the shoulder bone, the shoulder bone's connected to the head bone, all the live long day. Dem bones, dem bones, dem dry duck bones.

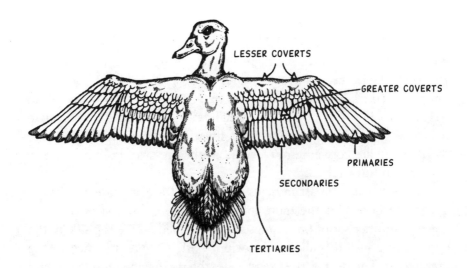

GENERAL FLIGHT DYNAMICS

Wings provide lift. The principle is that the higher the velocity of air passing over a surface, the lower the pressure on that surface.

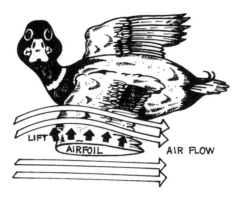

The air moving over the top of a wing has to move faster than the air below, and the greater pressure of the slower-moving air moving under the wing forces it upward, producing lift. Even ducks have a hard time understanding how this principle actually works but approaching Big Babe Lake, they are mighty pleased it does.

TAKING OFF

There are two different manners of taking off. Diver ducks take off like an airplane, running into the wind and accelerating along a water runway. Startled puddle ducks go straight up and out, like a helicopter. All takeoffs are energy intensive and use more than five times the energy needed to cruise. If spooked, ducks go potty at the same time, which is often the way a duck comments on your shooting ability.

FLYING

Climbing

On the down stroke, the wings move forward and down, with tight primaries twisting and pushing air, creating lift and forward motion. The secondaries don't move as much. On the upswing, wings move quickly back and up with primaries separated to reduce air resistance.

Turning

A duck turns by lowering a wing in the direction of turn, and raising and flapping the other wing hard. Turning would be easier if ducks had rudders on their tails but if they had all that equipment, they would be subject to FAA standards, and you know its record with small aircrafts.

Stalling

If ducks increase the angle of how the wind hits the leading edge of the wing, the air above the wing breaks away and swirls, and lift disappears, causing a stall. This is not done to frighten full-fare passengers—stalling is used to slow down. The reason why there are few fatal stalls is that ducks and geese have wing slots called "alulae" that automatically lift when the wings are in the stall position. The swift airflow through these narrow spaces on each wing is visible to anyone flying first cabin.

Racing

Ducks and geese leisurely cruise and migrate between forty and sixty miles an hour. Suitors that court and mate midair may need their turbo unit, which is located somewhere in the ventral area of the bird. When this unit is engaged, bird-watchers count the chunks in the vapor trail for their life book.

Gliding

If the bird has sufficient forward movement, enough lift is created to overcome gravity. Waterfowl gliding into your set of decoys have made an important commitment to you. Honor it!

THE FLOCK

Social animals that they are, ducks and geese like to fly together. Honkers like the V formation, sea ducks the long undulating wave, mergansers the single file, and mallards unimaginable flocks over Buck's blind. There are pseudoscientific reasons to fly together: for aerodynamics, to share information, or to baffle airborne predators. In formation, wing drag is distributed equally across all birds. When wings flap wing-tip-to-wing-tip, a pattern of air disturbance is created so trailing birds can use the spiraling air for lift, saving substantial energy.

The point or "lead" position is the most important appointment and traditionally goes to the most senior drake but more hens have been spotted taking the point, even as they fly in pairs. Members of the flock chatter in flight like pilots in a squadron, flashing bright speculums at one another. The staggered pattern of a formation allows the birds a clear forward view and avoids the unpleasantness associated with rear-end collisions.

SPECIAL WATERFOWL FLIGHT MANEUVERS

Evasion techniques were first developed after World War I. A small but determined group of American air defense artillerymen returned from Europe and formed a coastal defense group against the B-1s, the Flying Branta Canadensis Maximas, crossing the northern border to form pairs (and gain a valuable dual citizenship) with our native birds. Unfortunately, the Americans were trained by Brigitte Bardot, Goddess of the Hunt, on French guns. Many big birds got through, much to the continuing dismay of golf course operators in southernmost Minnesota.

In those early seasons, avian early-warning systems sounded when the first puffs of smoke, called Archies, appeared. The big birds would either suddenly bank 180 degrees to the left or right and/or drop a thousand feet. The first B-1s soon learned that single puffs meant single gun emplacements and avoided the barrage flak with many guns firing at one spot. Lesser brantas flying as escorts drew fire from the affected circles; casualties declined only when they flew routes through less fortified flyways or over Wisconsin.

LANDING

Once a duck has been cleared for landing, the bird slows and loses elevation by lowering its flaps, extending its primary landing gear or feet, and locking its leg tendons into position.

A big bird, like a goose or big fat park mallard, uses its big feet to steer and brake as well. If a bird has lowered the flaps too early, the wings are raised, spilling wind through the secondaries while the primary feathers hold lateral control.

When the bird nears the water with landing gear in place, the heels hit first. If the toes hit first, the juvenile flier will flip over, much to the delight of ducks already on the water.

CRASH LANDING

Once the birds are locked into Buck's sophisticated detection system and ground missiles have been launched with deadly accuracy, the birds' smooth flight is interrupted and they quickly lose elevation. If the autopilot is still functional, a larger bird will lock into a glide and become what is called a "sailer" in an extended swan dive. If all systems have shut down, the bird may either somersault forward and roll into a full gainer, or stall and fall and cannonball into the surf or turf. If the shooter was a nonresident, it's quite likely the bird was out of range and, while the duck may seem to be out of control, it's just experiencing a near-death experience.

EMBRACED BY THE FLIGHT

Minutes after being missed by nonresident steel shot, ducks have reported flying out of their bodies, rushing through dense fog via a dark passage to the Big Golden Marsh where they describe meeting Mother Goose, Daffy Duck, the Swan from Swan Lake, the Old Coot, and other spirit ducks.

This phenomenon of a fowl near-death experience or NDE is described as the duck seeming to step outside its body as it falls toward the water. An NDE can include a review of the panorama of its short life and the sighting of an intense light, a flash not unlike the muzzle blast of the second barrel. Comfort is offered by the appearance of the elders, Huey, Louie, and Dewey, in hooded brown robes; they guide the gentle supplicant through an intense review of past lives and a future of heavenly bliss.

Is this reported experience a psychological defense mechanism to a harsh reality, New Age hoo-ha, a physiological response by the small duck brain and nervous system to trauma from steel shot, or simply a case of rice bloat? It's difficult to say. In this limbo between life and death, ducks report experiencing a feeling of the peaceful hereafter, yet being able to overhear the commotion and view their bodies tumbling through the air. If the celestial jury of drakes determines that the duck must return to life to complete unfinished business, many ducks (especially thick-skinned sea ducks) experience sadness when returning to the waterfowling tradition, especially a tradition staffed by thick-skinned seaduck hunters.

The slap of cold water signals a return to the harsh realities of the duck world but NDE'ers are often transformed by their experiences, full of a new joy for life and compassion and unconditional love for all, even those in the blind below who will again bring them Nearer Thy Steel Shot To Thee.

CHAPTER 6

MIGRATIONS

The flight that engages waterfowl and waterfowlers is the annual migration. It wasn't always common knowledge that ducks and geese migrated. Roman naturalist Pliny the Elder was the first to ponder migratory habits as he drew a bead on Eider of the Briny. Aristotle the Dolt thought birds hibernated in the mud, which is another reason why he's not respected by the younger generation. By now almost everyone knows that ducks and geese take two major trips a year and these long-distance travels connect where they mate and where they incubate.

WHY DO DUCKS MIGRATE?
The politically correct answer to the above question is that the first migrations were stimulated by glacial spread and ducks were pushed out of the north by freezing waters and diminished food sources. When the Ice Age ended, the creatures of habit still went south for the winter and returned north in the spring to their homelands. The politically not-quite-as-correct answer is that ducks were once tropical and flew north for a cooler summer and returned south for the warmer weather.

The last two bar stools in the Valhalla Lounge at Buck's Duck Hunting Lodge have a decidedly politically incorrect theory. These evolutionists point out that the primitive walking drakes had sexual equipment that hung outside their body, playing an early role in steering (much like a ship's rudder) and as an external thermometer. Pushed by population growth, the pioneer birds had to compete for food and flew south for softer, less frozen landing strips.

This theory is supported by the separation of the central route to flyways that offer water landings. Government archaeologists have discovered the original flyway littered with evidence of painful landings; a collection of penal fossils is prominently displayed in the director's office in Washington, D.C. There are also several highly regarded Australian biologists (names and addresses withheld on their request) who further theorize that the drake's original hard landing created the hen.

WHAT INITIATES THE MIGRATION?

Ducks watch the constellations like old mariners. In the winter, the crisp cold skies easily reveal major navigational guideposts. In the northeast sky, the Big Dipper is rising and the leading edge of the dipper points toward the north star, Polaris, named after the hardy snow machines of northernmost Minnesota.

In the southern sky, Orion the Duck Hunter illuminates the darkness with his bright but now sagging belt of three stars, two starred shoulders and legs, and open breech.

Lying somewhere slavishly by his side is his retriever dog star, Sirius (Latin for "slavish dolt"), of the constellation Canis Major Anus (Latin) or Major Canis Anus (Greek). Above and to the front of Orion is the brightest star in the constellation Taurus the Ford, known primarily for its high resale value.

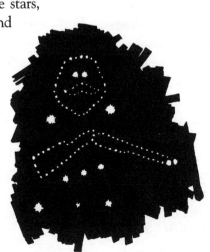

In the spring, Orion and his dolt dog move westerly until their bright stars disappear into the twilight. It's at this time that the senior avian air traffic controllers declare the coast clear for the return migration following a north star that is now directly below an inverted big dipper.

In the fall, waterfowl are spurred into flight by two celestial movements: the phenomena called the Harvest and Hunter's Moons. These bright waning moons rise at sunset in September and October to blur the already confusing closing hours and an ominous shift in constellations.

To the north, the Big Dipper is scraping the horizon from the west but in the south, Orion the Duck Hunter is closing the breech and his dolt dog has at least one eye open. Just before the breech closes, the highest-ranking officers in the duck force start their engines. There are several preliminary flights: In the fall, the drakes move from the nests to the molting areas and then on to a staging area. The hens follow once the kids are able to fly. In the spring, the pair move together from the breeding grounds to the staging area.

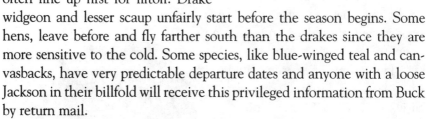

At the staging area, drakes often line up first for liftoff. Drake widgeon and lesser scaup unfairly start before the season begins. Some hens, leave before and fly farther south than the drakes since they are more sensitive to the cold. Some species, like blue-winged teal and canvasbacks, have very predictable departure dates and anyone with a loose Jackson in their billfold will receive this privileged information from Buck by return mail.

In the fall, the small and skinny birds move first because they are not dressed for the change of weather. The second and larger movement occurs at first freeze, signaled by the dumbest ducks touching tongues on metal signposts near the projects. The much smaller "un-movement" is by those birds whose personal gear is frozen in the ice. Except for that part of the fall migration that accelerates over Big Babe Lake, spring migrations are quicker in a race to get to the best breeding grounds.

There are runway problems as the flights begin, especially in overcrowded staging areas. On the runway, care is taken not to cross the long running divers with a group of vertical-lift puddlers. The first divers move into the take-off position with other high-priority migrants in close pursuit. True geese migrate in pairs and families and the immature won't take off without an elder to guide them, providing yet another reason for the harvest.

THE FLYWAYS

Once major liftoff has occurred, officials from the different waterfowl services send aircrafts into the air to guide the birds into the four principal flyways. Confirmed with banding information in the mid-thirties, these flyways are the principal administrative tool for the management of duck hunters as they blast away at ducks, geese, and swans following traditional routes to the wintering grounds. The four flyways funnel birds along state lines with the exception of the boundary between the Central and Pacific Flyways along the Continental Divide.

The Atlantic Flyway

The more mainland population of this flyway first appears as far west as the center of the Northwest Territories, and east to Baffin Island, Hudson Bay, the maritime coast, and Greenland, and moves across Lake Huron (avoiding Detroit International Airport at all costs) to meet the coastal group dipping their wings over the U.S. Fish and Wildlife Federal Beak Counting Center, and then on to the Big Bay and—following the East Coast—to the good life down in the Florida Keys.

The Mississippi Flyway

From all over the Northwest Territories, ducks and geese pour through all the provinces but British Columbia into a funnel over Big Babe Lake near the headwaters of the Mississippi. Newly widowed mallard hens continue downriver, over and through the bottoms of Illinois and Missouri, slowing over Arkansas to chuckle at the calling contests, and finally into the gumbo pots of Mississippi and Louisiana.

The Central Flyway

From the Northwest Territories down through Alberta, Montana, and Wyoming, this migration corridor funnels tons of birds on a very southerly route through pieces of New Mexico and Oklahoma, finally flaring across Texas (and Texans, to their continuing surprise) to settle from Corpus Christi to Houston on the Gulf Coast. Most of the Central Flyway species have recovered from Buck's early expeditions along the Snake River.

The Pacific Flyway

From the coasts of Alaska, tracking on two parallel paths, the eastern flight rubs the western edge of the Central Flyway and the western track follows the coast, flying over the ancestral home of the Intuits (a more insightful subgroup of the Inuits), grouping in southern Oregon, the central valley of California, and the Salton Sea of southern California before crossing the border into the land-without-limits.

HOW DUCKS STAY ON TRACK

The homing instinct is highest in mallards and widgeons and those birds heading home for the second time. It's weakest for pintails and the blue-winged devils (unless the little aces have been ordered back to headquarters).

Birds navigate by familiar natural and man-made landforms, echolocation, reading the southern and northern skies for different patterns of stars, and the sun's position in the sky. If they are heading south, they want the sun to set on their right wing. If they are moving east or west, in-flight collisions diminish when the sun has moved out of their direct path. There is evidence that ducks and geese orient by the earth's magnetic field. Research has discovered tiny crystals of a mineral known as magnetite in the heads of pigeons; it's thought they use the magnetic fields by taking a bearing on the angle between magnetic lines around the earth and vertical gravity. Researchers at Buck's Avian Research and Advanced Plucking Center have discovered substantial deposits of lead in juvenile birds hunted in Canada and these birds, along with those hobbled with leg bands, are at greatest risk from master hunters with magnetic personalities.

HOW HIGH, FAR, AND FAST?

Mallards have been struck at twenty-one thousand feet which is *not* information you'd share with a nonresident shooter carrying a new 10-gauge. Most ducks fly between three and four thousand feet with the majority migrating at night. Buck has seen geese over the lower Cascades at ten thousand feet but unfortunately the pilot wouldn't put the ol' goose hunter in range.

Ducks and geese can fly a thousand miles without stopping, swans farther. The longest migration, six thousand miles, may belong to the tundra swans but the pintail's trip of five thousand miles is nothing to be quacked at. Many ducks and geese shortstop in perfectly suitable habitat not quite so far away. Soon the agony of the long-distance flier may be for only those ducks wearing Nike wing tips.

On the spring migration, certain species of duck hens and a few geese fly pregnant and need to stop often to rest. Morning sickness causes some to throw up last night's rice or wild celery. The males are nearby but stay due north (and upwind) until their hens' "conditions" go away.

Waterfowl have three general speeds: lollygagging, general migrating, and turbo speed over Buck's blind and other hostile environments. Most ducks cruise at from forty to sixty miles per hour, Canada geese at about forty-five miles an hour. Black ducks poke along at thirty and, poked by a magnum load, a canvasback can ratchet up to eighty miles an hour. Buck has clocked a pair of mallards with the ol' Buckmobile at forty-six miles per hour. If they were flying much faster than that, it would have been hard to get a shot off and still stay on the road.

The migration is in every duck's blood. Daffy Duck finally headed south for the winter of 1952, but instead of flying, he hitchhiked. He, too, knew of the danger that lurked below.

PART TWO

THE DUCK HUNT

CHAPTER 7

DUCK HUNTING ESSENTIALS

Duck hunting is not like it was in Aldo Leopold's days when the makings of a duck hunter were "a stout heart, a pair of boots, and a gun." In the high-fashion world of the modern waterfowler, you need a very stout heart to afford a new pair of boots and a very stout wallet to afford a new gun.

CLOTHING
Buck suggests that the two best sources of duck hunting essentials for the serious waterfowler have been and can still be:

Someone Else
Someone else can be an older or younger brother, or an in-law who is bigger than you and newly married. The first condition needs no explanation. Your success from the second is determined by how close you park to the garage door as the new spouse pushes or, depending on how things are going, pitches out bachelor boy toys. Since your father may still be your hunting partner, another good prospect is a retired grandfather, the preferred source of heavily oiled cotton clothes that are finally soft goods.

The U.S. Military
The standard-issue M65 army field coat was Buck's first serious hunting jacket. His second serious hunting jacket was a tailored olive drab jacket with the camouflaged insignias of the Vietnam era. Even Buck's jump primaries were dark. The problem with today's uniforms is

that wetland camouflage isn't being designed for the international sand traps of our national interest. New and used "old" military gear is easy to find in surplus stores.

OTHER CLOTHING
Cap or Hat

For the early season, Buck wears a sorta waterproof baseball cap. For the late season, he wears a 100 percent virgin worsted wool hat with flaps, which provokes snickers from the blind until the snickerers' bulky bodies cool down from the walk in. For the entire season, Buck recommends that all in or near his blind on Big Babe Lake wear protective helmets tested to withstand direct hits from a sky that will seem like it's falling.

Pants

Buck recommends wool for all outdoor activities and prefers trousers made of the heaviest of malone cloths, thirty ounces of handsome dark gray wool with faint red overplaid. A synthetic shell is put over the pants for high-wind conditions or to disappear in a snow field. Newer wool garments are lightly mixed with "miracle" fibers; the feel still reminds you of Buck's 100 percent wool garments that not only kept you warm but scratched in all the right places.

Underwear

The most important piece of underwear for both the youngest and oldest waterfowler seeing the Blue-winged Devils for the first time is not the availability of high-tech underwear systems but the availability of adult-sized diapers.

IMPORTANT REMINDER: Diaper-sizing information refers to the weight of the occupant, not the maximum carrying capacity of the material.

Footwear

To reach duck-only areas by foot, some hunters use nine-foot-long, six-and-one-half-inch-wide marsh skis. The late, great George Herter recommended building your own six-foot-long, twelve-inch-wide and -deep bog shoes. Buck prefers to hunt late-winter river bottom ducks on snowshoes. Waterproof footwear comes in three significant lengths:

chest waders, hip boots, and short boots. Waders are best when the water under your decoy spread is over your waist and/or you need a place to warm your sandwiches. Hip boots are best when your partner has waders and you don't have a wet boat seat to worry about. Short boots belong back at the lodge.

Clothing is the smaller part of a duck hunter's budget unless you fall victim to camo confusion. There are camouflage patterns for each type of duck habitat and the need to dress smartly and look prettier than the next hunter has its price. Even the minor items such as shotgun shells and decoys are not exempt from seasonally inflated needs. License prices have stayed sorta flat but they're cleverly made with extra room for special-purpose stamps. It's in the arena of major boy toys such as shotguns, boats, and retrievers that egos are really massaged to buy bigger, better, and faster.

SHOTGUNS

To duck hunt, you'll need a shotgun. All other types of firearms are illegal or wrong. Shotguns come in all sizes and shapes.

Single-Barrel Shotguns
Advantage: Less costly.
Disadvantage: Less costly, but why spend *less* on a hunting essential?

Single-Shot Shotgun
Advantages: Highly reliable, very cheap.
Disadvantages: Cheap, one shot, one choke. A bolt action will shoot more than one shell but it's still one at a time.

Pump-Action Shotgun
Advantages: Reliable, cheap, and available with bottom ejection. Sourdough's first duck gun was the classic Winchester Model 97. Porky Pig chose a pump for hunting Daffy Duck.
Disadvantages: Pumping may interrupt a swing. Some shooters lift their heads before or during a pump and aim too high. Only one choke. To the duck's disadvantage, Sourdough's first duck gun was the classic Winchester Model 97. To Daffy's advantage, Porky's pump jammed.

Automatic Shotgun
Advantages: Three legal shots, less recoil.
Disadvantages: If not cleaned religiously, subject to malfunction and again one shot. Still one choke, unless a variable choke is installed. The classic is the Browning Model 5 but Buck's Winchester Model 50 was best for ducks and is still mighty fine on sandy-colored furbearers.

Double-Barrel Shotguns
Advantages: Two chokes, no wasted third shot, and no swing-interrupting activity. Fewer moving parts. Shorter by almost three inches than autoloaders of same barrel length. Shells are easier to collect. Easier to clean. No powder residue blow-by on a left-handed shooter's face. Easy to see down barrels for obstructions.
Disadvantages: Only two shots. Elmer Fudd tried to blast Daffy Duck with a side-by-side and he obviously could have used the third shot of an automatic. High cost per ounce.

Over-Under Shotgun
Advantages: Single barrel sighting plane. Pretty.
Disadvantage: High cost per ounce.

Side-By-Side Shotgun
Advantages: Doesn't need to be broken open so far. Very pretty.
Disadvantage: High cost per ounce.

PERFORMANCE EXTRAS

Back Boring
Overboring or increasing the inside diameter or bore of the barrel is done to lower pressure (thus recoil), which squeezes lead pellets (altering patterns) at long range. Back boring is less necessary with the harder steel shot; too much back boring may have steel pellets escaping the petals of a wad and scouring the interior of an expensive bore.

Forcing Cones
The part of the barrel that tapers from the chamber to the standard diameter of the barrel is the forcing cone. The longer the cone, the less pressure and recoil. Experts say longer cones don't actually lessen recoil

since steel doesn't deform as easily as lead. The felt recoil is noticeably greater when the cost of installing custom forcing cones is revealed.

Porting

Porting the business end of the upper barrel lets gases escape early, forcing the barrel downward and thus reducing muzzle rise. Porting is advertised to noticeably reduce perceived recoil on single-barrels and the first barrel of a double. One patented process "consists of eleven compound ellipsoidal ports on each side of the barrel." Buck's unpatented process consists of nine oval ports in the shape of his after-the-hunt face. When smoke pours out these holes, the visage of a great and powerful Norwegian prince appears, which is sorta true.

SOME QUESTIONS ABOUT SHOTGUNS

Which Brand Shotgun Should You Buy?

All name-brand shotgun manufacturers make safe guns. Not all make pretty ones. Buy the one that makes you feel pretty!

Which Brand Shotgun Does Buck Own?

Buck's first and still best shotgun is a Winchester Model 50, bought the same year as his first federal duck stamp. He uses it anywhere lead shot is sold and shot. It's the same gun Nash Buckingham customized; Buck plans to refit the old classic for steel and, if he's feeling really flush, add a ventilated rib and a little bluing on the interchangeable barrels. He won't do much to the stock, a little linseed oil maybe. His saltwater gun is the cheapest Remington 870 on the market. His duck hunting partner shoots an older, deluxe 870 to great effect.

What Size Shotgun Should You Buy?

Most duck hunters pop primers through 12-gauge barrels. Some very good (and junior and lady) shooters shoot the light and nimble 20-gauge. Gauge is the measuring unit of the bore of a shotgun and is based on the number of lead balls of that bore diameter that make a pound. A 12-gauge means twelve pure lead balls of .729-inch diameter (the actual bore diameter of a 12-gauge) weigh one pound. Ed Zern suggested that a 12-gauge designation refers to the number of lead balls required to make an even dozen. Since U.S. Fish and Wildlife now allows only the use of steel shot, bore measurements based on obsolete lead weights have made your fine double-barrel shotguns obsolete and possibly dangerous and they should immediately be sent to Buck in care of the publisher for disposal.

SHOULD YOU BUY A NEW OR USED SHOTGUN?

A similar question is, should you buy a new or used (and possibly dangerous) duck boat? If you buy new, should you buy off the shelf or custom-fitted? Excuse me! Is that a question? If you decide on a custom gun (which you so rightfully deserve), you'll need to know things like length of pull, drop at the comb and heel, and cast and pitch. If you don't have those personal measurements handy, custom gun makers can estimate those critical dimensions from the following: distance between the eyes, distance from the top of your shooting shoulder to the bottom of your ear, distance from the front to the back of your wallet, and general conformation of shoulders, facial structure, cheekbones, and, most important, backbone.

If you plan to buy a new custom gun, determine how much cash you have to spend. If you are short and you will be, other cash sources are:

>   your spouse's checking account;
>
>   your spouse's savings account;
>
>   your children's trust funds;
>
>   your children's college fund;
>
>   your checking account;
>
>   your savings account.

If that is still not enough and it won't be, acting as a legal guardian, sign your mother-in-law as an organ donor to a private institution and commit her heart (if available) for cash. Her most used parts (and we know which ones *those* are) have little value.

Buck will buy a new-to-him shotgun when he hits all he can with his current guns. Which could be tomorrow. Or was yesterday.

THE FUTURE OF SHOTGUNS

The trend for many insecure hunters is toward larger guns. You have to go to a museum or to England to see one of the really big guns, the 4- and 8-gauge blunderbusses of the market hunters and the 2- and 4-gauge punt guns mounted on a double-pointed skiff that blow out a pound of BBs, dropping a hundred birds in one fell swoop. Sensing yet another marketing opportunity with the dissatisfaction with steel shot, gun manufacturers now sell three-and-one-half-inch 12-gauge and 10-gauge sky blasters. Big gun people have told Buck on the QT that there is no muzzle end in sight. Gun designers have larger gauges on the boards, including an on-the-shoulder weapon, shown below (please look quickly as these secret sketches have to be returned before Monday).

SHOTGUN SHELLS

Once upon a time, you could let lead fly at ducks and geese. Now you have to shoot feathered flying objects with steel pellets. Steel performs differently than lead and the differences are accommodated in the construction of the shot shell.

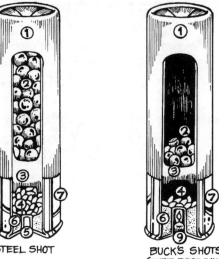

LEAD SHOT   **STEEL SHOT**   **BUCK'S SHOTS**
(ON THE FIRST DAY) (OF THE SEASON)

1. TUBE	4. POWDER	7. HEAD
2. SHOT	5. PRIMER	8. CUSHION (LEAD SHOT ONLY)
3. WAD	6. BASE WAD	9. CANDLE (BUCK'S SHOTS ONLY)

THE OLD LEAD SHELL

With compressible wad or shot cup to dampen shock and thus reduce pellet deformation.

THE STEEL SHELL

With no compression of steel shot, the space is taken with more shot.

BUCK'S SHOT

On the first day of the season, a candle primer, and too few powder and shell particles.

All shot shells come with the above parts. The important buying decisions are concerned with:

Size

Shells are measured from the base to the edge of the opened crimp. To be sure of receiving advertised value, measure your cases once fired and on the ground. The sure measure of the owner of the shell is determined by what else is on the ground.

Dram Equivalent

A meaningless term that compares the velocity of modern powder to black powder. As applied to a duck hunter from Wisconsin, the term refers to the number of alcoholic beverages consumed in the Lodge.

There are dram shot laws that limit how many drams of spirits you can have before you fall down and break something.

Lead or Steel

You have no choice in the United States. You must shoot steel. In Canada and Mexico, you can shoot most anything else and most non-residents do. Steel is required because ducks can't pass lead pellets. When lead is ground in a duck's gizzard, the residue kills the bird. Steel is three times harder than lead and when the gizzard finally figures that out, the shot is quickly pushed toward the rear exit. Shooters using steel point slightly less ahead of a bird under thirty yards, slightly more at greater distances. Many shooters complain that steel cripples too many birds, especially if shot as lead. It's hard to get the lead out of these shooters.

Entrepreneurs are experimenting with other metals to produce the nontoxic shell of the future. Copper is too toxic, iron too hard, and gold too expensive. Shot made of 97 percent bismuth and 3 percent tin is attracting attention. Bismuth is the active ingredient in Pepto-Bismol; unfortunately, early studies show that swallowing a box of the experimental shells will not relieve the stomach distress brought on by tavern food. Bismuth is softer and more malleable for old gun barrels and is, in fact, recommended for use by one of the most respected custom gun makers, whose prices are the cause of much spousal indigestion. The first round of toxicity tests of bismuth on ducks have been successful. In the first thirty-day study, the most significant finding was that the gonads of bismuth-dosed ducks weighed less than those of ducks dosed by steel shot. Another significant finding in the laborious application and testing process was that the gonads of the shooters developing bismuth shot were significantly larger than those of the officials who kept saying no.

VERY IMPORTANT QUESTIONS ABOUT SHOTGUN SHELLS

Which shotgun shells should you use?

Your hunting partner's, of course! It's much cheaper and if you miss with those shells, you can blame your pal for buying the wrong steel shot for the high-test leaded conditions.

Which shotgun shells should you buy?

It doesn't make much difference as the bullet boys all make about the same shells. Each has a distinctive color. Buck shoots a lot of shells from his home state of Minnesota because the rich red color of the shells matches his eyes at o-dark thirty in the morning.

THE MOST IMPORTANT QUESTION ABOUT SHOTGUN SHELLS

How many should you pack?

The average for most residents is three shells per duck. Buck's seasonal average is three ducks per shell. His lifetime average is even better. The average for nonresidents is more, considerably more. Puddle ducks take fewer shells, bay ducks more, and sea ducks many more. Some shooters use an average of three shells to drop a sea duck to the water, ten shells to try to put the bird away while on the water, one more shell at the blind, and one outside the kitchen.

DUCK BOATS

The choices depend on whether you use a boat to shoot from or to carry you and your equipment to a blind or both.

Canoe

The primary transportation of Native Americans, trappers, and French voyeurs, the canoe is light, versatile, and small enough to be put on a car. Buck's first (and best) duck (and turtle) hunting boat was a seventeen-foot-square stern fiberglass canoe made by Herter's, the original Minnesota outfitter. Buck's second best duck hunting boat was the canoe owned and expertly guided by Buck's elk hunting buddy on an icy Snake River for late-winter ducks. The bayou version of a canoe is the pirogue. Originally carved out of a single cypress log, this long, slim, double-pointed, flat-bottomed boat is thought to be so sensitive that Nash Buckingham told occupants to "shift your chewing gum or change your mind in a 'pee-roog' and see what happens."

Johnboat

While its origins are not too clear, it is known that there was a fellow named John who owned a wide, flat-bottomed boat that was stable and easy to transport. Even though it was cheap and easy enough for others to build, his neighbors and friends were always hounding John to use his boat. A rumored slightly slower brother, Ralph, had an idea for a similar boat. As expected, it came out much later and a good thing as the boat type would have become a ralphboat, a name already in use for well-stocked party boats on choppy seas.

Layout Boats

Big-water (bigger than Big Babe Lake) duck boats often come in pairs, with one larger boat towing a flat one-person layout boat into position among the decoys. Usually less than ten feet long and about four feet wide and a foot deep, the small gunning rigs are anchored and the shooter's back is on the bow. With only a few inches of freeboard, stiff skiff occupants make sure the big warm safe boat is always in sight. The majority of the body must be out of water for the boat to avoid being classified as a sinkbox, a classic now outlawed in the States. This floating coffin had a deck weighted by iron decoys and connected to hinged wings that moved with the waves.

BUCK'S IMPORTANT HISTORICAL NOTE: The sinkbox is the smaller, open version of the gunning party boat that saw usage in the barely civil war between the duck clubs of the North and South. The salient issue in this conflict was whether black ducks used as live decoys (called "Suzies") should be set free after long and faithful employment. The most famous duck boat of this period was the *Monitor*.

An experimental boat with one shotgun turret on a raft that floated just eighteen inches above the water, the *Monitor* was deployed to teach the southern end of the Atlantic Flyway some manners and secure some semblance of order in the famed hunting grounds of Chesapeake Bay. On March 9, 1862, the *Monitor* made an ironclad case for the northern waterfowlers.

You need not look far for a boat that works for duck hunting. Clean out the fishhooks and petrified worms in the bottom of your V-hulled wall-eye boat or remove the bright Cinzano umbrellas from the deck of your pontoon boat and cover either with camouflage yard goods. Buck's new marsh boat is a flat ten-foot fiberglass skiff, big enough to hold a half-dozen decoys and a picture of a slightly disappointed Dorothy wishing the occupant godspeed in his new small quarters.

DECOYS

Decoys have become such an integral piece of waterfowling equipment that it's easy to assume that imitations were always used to attract game birds. That's not true. The word *decoy* is thought to have come from a Dutch word for a netted box that wildfowl were driven into; live birds, "Suzies" or "stool pigeons," were tied to wooden frames or "stools" to decoy wild birds into range. The term *stools* is now used interchangeably with *decoy sets*, except when describing the awfulness produced by one of Buck's hunting buddies after eating green eggs and ham for breakfast.

History
One of the first decoys was discovered in Nevada's Lovelock Cave in 1911. Made of tule rush, covered with skins and feathers, these decoys are thought to have been used over a thousand years ago by a group of Indian hunters called the Tule Eaters. The decoying ducks came stuffed with tule weed, saving time in the cave kitchens for the Tule chefs. What's notable is that this decoy was more advanced than a mound of mud deco-rated with a stick head, certainly not something you would expect from someone living so far out in the tules.

   The first modern decoys were lifelike and made of cork, wood, and canvas. When was the inflatable rubber duck first introduced? Hard to say.

It's one of those duck-and-egg questions. They probably showed up on both big open water and small bathtub water at roughly the same time. When larger sets were needed on both land and water, silhouettes gained popularity. On salt water, seaduck silhouettes were nailed together like small catamarans.

Decoys now come in all sizes and shapes and are made of different types of material. After extensive research into the size of hunter billfolds, decoy manufacturers now offer three decoy sizes: the sixteen-inch standard, the eighteen-inch oversized, and the magnum twenty-one-inch duck decoy. Wild birds of other lengths will just have to land in Buck's odd-sized, homemade wooden deeks. Most early decoys portrayed heads-up, alert birds. Now many of them look like dolt park birds, sleeping and eating. Buck's homemade deeks portray ducks just happy to be ducks.

Mass-market decoys are made of synthetic materials. The field preferences for old-timers like Buck are handmade wooden decoys. He and his brothers have gunnysacks of cedar body/pine head decoys; the mallards and bluebills sport Herter's brightest colors. Second choice is wood-gunning deeks made by friends. Third and the most expensive choice is factory-made wooden decoys. Whether it be balsa, cork, or a selected hard/softwood, wood has the heft to ride like a duck body in water and the density to continue floating after nonresidents blast it.

SOME QUESTIONS ABOUT DECOYS
What Size Decoy Should You Use?
There are two schools of thought on the proper size of decoys. Some think oversized imitations attract more attention and others prefer the realism of life-sized birds. There is a gut pile of meaningless chatter on these choices. If the skybusters downwind are using standard-sized decoys, will birds engaged in a steep vertical ascent see, much less care, to land in your larger decoys? No! Buck prefers using a substandard-sized decoy to imitate the runts of the litter who appreciate the special attention. To shock the nonresident collectors staying at his Lodge, Buck really enjoys shooting over mantelpiece decoys.

What Decoy Rigging Should You Use?
Buck's decoys have anchors of chunks and hunks of steel and iron. Bolts, lug nuts, and even a few door hinges from the garage have worked for over thirty years. Several kinds of cords are popular: monofilament,

braided nylon, parachute cord, and commercial tangle-free line. All work well. Some old-timers used to tar decoy lines. Wrap the anchor line twice through ring or hole before securing with a bowline knot.

What Species Decoy Should You Use?

Most shooters use decoys that imitate birds they hope to attract. Some diver ducks, especially bluebills, will come into puddler decoys. Puddle ducks prefer not to drop into diver blocks and when you look at some of those odd divers, you can't wonder why. Old-timers like using what's called a confidence decoy, an imitation blue heron or even black duck, to show the birds above that even the most skittish feel safe here. The Buckster, mythical warrior, master oyster shooter, and senior ceremonial dancer of the Intuits, hunts over his hand-carved Old Coot decoy.

All he needs is one. In one of the few extended families that still pay respect to their elders, coots (and other friends) will gather around the old coot to learn of the old ways and the old days.

What Sex Decoy Should You Use?

Early in the season Buck may use only hen decoys for birds still in eclipse plumage. Most species, especially the juveniles, have a roughly even mix of drakes and hens so Buck puts out a similar mix on the water to attract the later flocks. Since Buck only shoots magnum drake mallards, he has designed and trademarked a decoy that catches the big greenheads by the curly coverts.

Some say modeled after the head bartender of the Valhalla Lounge, The Bawdy Duck® is a magnum mama, a bog babe, all decked out with rosy red lips, blue eye shadow, and a more-than-ample bosom. If drake mallards had pinup calendars, The Bawdy Duck® would be the cover girl.

To stimulate big drakes into thinking there is some treading action available on the water, rig the decoy starting with a line from shore, down through an anchor on the bottom, and up and tied to a hole in the middle of the keel. Pulling the string, the bird goes flat in the water, waiting for a suitor. For fun, Buck waits until the drake bites The Bawdy Duck® in the back of the neck before pulling the hen down to the bottom. Drakes don't like being caught with their coverts down!

HOW TO RIG THE BAWDY DUCK®

BUCK'S BONUS TIP: One of Buck's most secret sets of decoys is his little ducklings. Arranged in a small string just far enough out from the blind to suggest that the deeks are orphans, Buck's Lil' Ducks are irresistible to a female empty-nester and her suitors.

To make a set of six decoys, Buck's Lil' Ducks pattern may be used at no extra cost to the reader. Cut and shape the body out of cedar, the head out of pine, and use ⅜″ dowel to secure the head to the body. The finished product should measure approximately five inches long and be painted a golden yellow with dark spots.

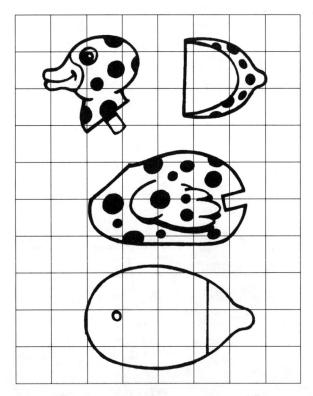

BUCK'S EXTRA BONUS TIP: Screw an extra eyelet in the stern of the bottom of the decoy and attach a treble hook like an ol' cree-duk lure to engage any troublesome bass or northern pike.

DUCK BLINDS

The blind was originally used to hide from the prehistoric ancestors of the duck. Early waterfowlers hid underground in limestone caves and painted great tales of imaginary hunts. A critical point in the development of the sport occurred when an ancient waterfowler realized that if he just hid from ducks, he'd never be able to see and shoot them. Less-than-perfect blinds have been the standard since.

There are two basic types of blinds: portable and permanent. Portable blinds can be as simple and impromptu as camouflage cloth draped between four-foot poles or a white tarp pulled over a depression in a snow-covered cornfield. You may not even need a portable blind, just someplace to get out of the direct view of a wary game bird. Buck and his brother-in-law have spent many early mornings in the ditch up against the roadbed waiting to blast a duck coming off McCormic Lake. Buck and his brother have hidden behind trees in Arkansas, waiting for fat greenheads to drop through the "hole." Some large water shooters "boot" ducks by hiding behind a large goose decoy in the middle of a wader-deep spread. Surf shooters just hide among the rocks.

Permanent blinds are not permanent but they seem more substantial. The easiest and least expensive route is to occupy nonthreatening structures already in the field, such as by standing in a haystack or inside a channel marker.

Below-the-ground blinds have a wider application. For example, saltwater bay blinds may be as simple as oil drums sunk into the tide flats.

On dry ground in open fields, Buck prefers the coffin blind, a made-to-fit box that is dug deep enough in field stubble so the top of the coffin is at the same level as the surrounding stubble. Used metal coffins should be sanded and painted to match the habitat and all hinges oiled on a regular basis.

The difficulty with the more complicated structures is that Dorothy can't or won't feel comfortable in them and that is as good a reason as any to use only simple marsh grass blinds, such as those around Big Babe Lake.

BUCK'S SPECIAL BLIND TIP: Other than a converted Minnesota fish house, the best above-ground blind is a porta-potty. Now that the Occupational Safety and Health Administration requires toilets within range of all the outdoor trades, it's not difficult to pick up a used blind at a reasonable price. The advantages are many: You don't need a refuge building permit, a double-holer can be shared, and no self-respecting duck would believe you are inside.

CHAPTER 8

REGULATIONS

Before decisions can be made on how many birds you can blast into orbit, flocks of biologists or recruitment boards migrate to Canada and other prairie pothole nesting grounds to spend their spring and summer vacations counting nesting ponds, the number of breeding pairs, and little beaks. Young birds born in the spring and counted in the summer are called the recruitment.

Juvenile birds that don't want to be on the federal register glide quietly over the international border at night to avoid the draft of those who rush to be counted. The recruitment plus adult birds make up the entire avian air force. The data is collected in several ways:

Aerial Visual Counts

Flights over preselected transects are used to actually count the birds on the ground. Once the numbers get too high, video and still cameras are used for the bill counters back at the office.

Ground Visual Counts

A smaller number of birds is counted in these areas at the same time of the day. In the early days, counts taken in the late afternoon seemed to contain some of the same beaks from the early-morning count.

Ground Call-Response Counts

Old duck callers and retired project managers are recruited to call into the marsh with a specialized how-many-are-you? call perfected by

the U.S. Census Bureau, inner city division. This call stimulates shy and unsuspecting ducks to answer the roll call.

The borderline teams leave the north country when they have gathered the necessary data or can't gulp down one more Canadian pale ale, whichever comes first or last. This information is added to the individual state surveys, hunter reports, and January waterfowl count and given to the four American flyway councils that meet in late summer to have more beer and chips. Representatives from each council then migrate to Washington for martinis and hors d'oeuvres with the National Flyway Council and all the collected data is used to predict the fall flight.

Recommendations for seasons and limits are then made to the Department of the Interior for an allowable harvest that would still leave enough breeders to return in the spring, to continue building toward a goal of millions of breeding birds and a fall flight of even more millions of ducks.

How are seasons really set? Does the Secretary of the Interior rule on recommendations that originate from flyway committees made up of local waterfowl managers making rational, scientific decisions? That's sorta true.

In northernmost Minnesota, the local waterfowl managers meet at the end of the season in the Valhalla Lounge to count the leg and neck bands and the curled covert feathers entered in the Boom and Crockpot Club. Once that information has been collated, which takes the better part of happy hour, the district oomancer of the U.S. Fish and Wildlife Service cracks a fresh duck egg and drops the contents into a bowl of marsh water to divine the shape of the season to come. If the yolk splits, so does the season.

What is certain in any new year is that Buck's Dead Duck Society will enroll another full recruitment of drake mallards. If the council wants to keep at least seven million mallards in the pipeline, they must consider this extraordinary draft. The allowable harvest is the base population plus the average harvest by average hunters, the guaranteed harvest by the Society, an estimate of crippling by nonresidents, and mortality from predation. On Big Babe Lake, the average resident harvest is the number of drake mallards allowed times the number of days in the season. The nonresident harvest, if any, is still being calculated (it can be assumed both additive and compensatory—all real ducks survive at a high shooter out-of-pocket cost). There is no predation near Buck's blinds because he shoots and eats raccoons. In fact, if a reader has a loose Jackson in the billfold, Buck will send on his favorite predator recipes. He live-traps skunks and releases them under the local Finnish Dance Hall to mingle freely with the scent of old-fashioned personal hygiene almost trapped in wool union suits. Seasons are set on all species in each flyway in a similar manner, with considerations for any special shooting preserves like Big Babe Lake. If officials know Buck and other key members of the Dead Duck Society are planning to hunt other flyways, the affected regional council adjusts its sustainable harvest accordingly.

FOR THE CONVENIENCE OF DEAD DUCK SOCIETY MEMBERS AND GUESTS

A SUMMARY OF FEDERAL REGULATIONS

Full and complete regulations are kept in bound buckram on the back bar in the Vallhalla Lounge, next to the hard-boiled eggs.

No Person Shall Take Migratory Game

with trap, snare, net, rifle, pistol, swivel gun, shotgun with a barrel larger than a bread box, crossbow, punt gun, battery gun, battery-operated gun, machine gun, anti-aircraft gun, bazooka, fishhook, heavy explosive, poison, drug, or any of the other stupefying substances commonly found in a duck camp.

with any shotgun capable of holding more than three shells, unless plugged with a one-piece filler that is incapable of being removed without disassembling the gun and losing many of the parts.

from a sinkbox or any low-floating device having a depression, affording the hunter means of concealment beneath the surface of the water and the ability to still stay sorta dry.

by use or aid of live birds as decoys. Live birds used for species identification must be kept inside the blind and quiet.

from or by means of any motorboat or sailboat unless the motor and any motormouths in the boat have been completely shut off and/or the sail unfurled and progress therefore ceased. Grog must be securely stored before the officials board or ram the boat.

using records, tapes, or CDs of migratory birdcalls, or electronically amplified imitations of birdcalls. Birdcalling by Wisconsin hunters along their side of the St. Croix or Mississippi River may be prosecuted to the full extent under the Minnesota Clean Air Act.

by diving, rallying, or chasing birds to put them in range with any motorized conveyance including non-club-owned submarines and pontoon boats, or any nonmotorized conveyance including sailboats.

by the aid of baiting (placing feed such as corn, wheat, salt, or other feed to constitute a lure or enticement) on or over any baited area, or by the aid of placing decoy Wisconsin shooters in or near the blind. Hunters should be aware that a baited area is considered to be baited for ten days after removal of the bait and it is not necessary for the hunter to know an area is baited to be in violation, especially if the hunter is a nonresident.

Steel Shot

No person shall take ducks, geese, swans, or coots while possessing shot shells loaded with shot other than steel shot, or such shot approved as nontoxic, unless approved by calling the game warden at home after dark.

Closed Season

No person shall take migratory game birds during the closed season whenever that is.

Shooting or Hawking Hours

No person shall take migratory game birds except during the hours open to shooting hawks as prescribed.

Daily Bag Limit

No person shall take in any one day more than one daily bag limit unless he/she has a really large bag.

Field Possession Limit

No person shall possess while in the field, have in custody, or transport more than one daily bag limit between the place where taken and either:

his/her automobile or principal means of land transportation;

his/her personal abode or temporary place of lodging;

a migratory bird preservation facility;

a post office or federal migratory express drop box;

a common carrier facility (whatever a common carrier is); or

an Environment Canada diplomatic pouch.

Other Possession

No person shall possess more than one daily limit on the opening day of the season, unless that dark voice in the back of your head told you it's okay.

No person shall possess more than the possession limit unless local customs dictate that ten-ninths possession is nine-tenths of the law.

No person, including commercial facilities, shall possess migratory birds of another person unless such birds are tagged by the taker with the total number of birds and species, and the date killed, and signed with at least an X or a nose print by the taker.

No person shall give, put, or leave any migratory game birds at any place or in the custody of another person unless the birds are tagged by the hunter with the following information: the hunter's signature, the hunter's address, the estimated total number of birds involved, the species, the dates such birds were thought to be killed, and a small gift for the uniformed inspector.

All wounded migratory game birds shall be retrieved, if possible, and retained in the custody of the hunter in the field. Wounded small birds should be given emergency care and then floated upwind of a neighbor's blind. Wounded big birds shall be immediately killed and included in the daily bag limit.

Trespassing

Federal law prohibits unauthorized trespass on Native American-owned reservations for hunting, fishing, or trapping purposes. Trespass to gamble is permitted, but not recommended.

Dual Violations

Violation of state migratory bird regulations is also a violation of federal regulations and, if you are a nonresident, that's three strikes and you're out, mister.

A SUMMARY OF STATE REGULATIONS

Residents get to shoot first.

Seasons and Bag Limits

Ducks, Coots, and Mergansers: October 1 to 2, November 26 to 26½, December 25, and anytime after 11 P.M. on December 31. Sea Ducks: October 2 to February 15.

Duck Limits

The weekly bag limit of ducks may include no more than one hen mallard, one pintail, two wood ducks, one black duck, two redheads, one brunette, and one fulvous partridge in a pear tree. The possession limit is twice the square root of the above.

Exceptions: Blue-winged and green-winged teal shall be allowed to be shot at during the month of October with a daily miss limit of two each in addition to the regular miss limit on ducks. The taking of sea ducks in Minnesota, except during regular duck season, shall be limited to state salt waters. The seaduck limit of eight daily or a thousand in possession may be taken in addition to the limits prescribed for regular duck season.

Daily Bag Limit

The daily bag limit is based on the point system. The daily limit is reached when the point value for the last duck taken, added to the sum of the point value for ducks already taken, reaches or exceeds 100 points U.S. or 1,000 Canadian. With the exception of the lowly coot, the aggregate shall not exceed five birds; more than five birds aggravates the warden, another old coot.

Waterfowl Point Values

100 points
>One black duck
>One nursing female mallard

70 points
>One redhead
>One wood duck
>One hooded merganser
>One dry female mallard

35 points
>One male mallard
>One pintail
>One bufflehead and most other ducks not listed
>One old-maid female mallard

20 points
>One widgeon
>One teal in under fifteen shots

05 points
>One hundred coots
>One nonresident Styrofoam decoy

Shooting Hours

No dawn busting. No dusk busting.

Except for opening day when the season starts at noon or lunch, whichever comes first, the legal shooting hours start thirty minutes after sunrise and end when the face on your smiling black Labrador loses definition.

Areas Open To Hunting

The Warden's Wildlife Management Area: Beginning at the refuse container nearly a half mile southwest of Nick Lyons' Book, Bullet, and Bait Shop then west and north on country road 27 to the junction of section 72 east, township 27 north, range 72 north by northwest as the

Hitchcock flies. Then 272 yards south to the high-water line on the east bank of The River Runs Through It, then east to the sleeping Indian behind tepee door number 4, then south on the 2700 West Road to the 7200 North Road, then east in an easterly fashion to the northwest corner of Ben's outhouse, then south and west to the scarecrow in the alfalfa field, then north or south—it doesn't make any difference—following the barbed fence line that runs north to the game warden's favorite donut shop, then east toward widow Wanda's barn where all those shenanigans took place a few years ago, then south to a point due west that is 250 hectares (Canadian) north of the low-water mark of the natural hot springs where all those hippie women bathe and where Jed embarrassed his self, then taking your compass and following due magnetic south until you feel the unbearable lightness of just being there.

Special Regulations

With the exception of those born under the sign of Orion the hunter, all hunters must possess proof of the successful completion of a hunter education course. Those under ten are exempt but must be accompanied by an adult who is registered to vote but probably doesn't.

Non-Native Camo Requirements

Every nonresident hunter during a waterfowl season shall wear a hat or upper body clothing of at least 100 square inches of a camo pattern not native to the area that can be visible to game wardens and other resident poachers from 360 degrees.

Clubhouse Rules

No guest privileges on Saturday, Sunday, or any other day that lots of birds are flying.

LICENSES AND STAMPS

All hunters must have in possession all or some of the below:

Resident Basic License

This is the lowest-priced full privilege hunting permit.

BUCK'S SPECIAL NOTE: This is the license that out-of-state rascals try to buy in trusting small-town hardware stores, claiming their driver's license was lost in a DWI conviction. Innocent clerks acknowledge the possibility just by the looks of the applicant and accept a passport issued in that state as proof of residence.

Resident Senior License

The reduced price balances the wisdom with the infirmities of age.

Resident Senior Lifetime License

Combined with the bearer of a junior license who can identify species and sex, this license can have a rich, full life.

Resident Junior Under Fifteen License

This license doesn't require a federal duck stamp but that doesn't mean they won't require a junior duck stamp at a future date. Occasionally a youth goose hunting permit is issued to thin the ranks of resident honkers, which is a good thing.

Nonresident Three-Day License

This license acknowledges that most nonresidents require three days to take one day's limit.

Nonresident Basic License

For all the right reasons, this license is the single most expensive license. On Big Babe Lake, even the Sons of Knute are nonresidents and Buck and Babe intend to keep it that way, especially after the embarrassing shied-poke incident.

State Stationary Duck Blind License For Riparian Owners

Some states require this special license but only if you are a proud owner of a riparian. *Warning!* If you have been convicted of a felony, you cannot vote, run for elective office, or even own a riparian. The more expensive stationary duck blind license for non–riparian owners is the only option for a convicted felon. No exceptions except for those who can produce evidence of riparian deprivation.

State Floating Blind License

Some states require a license should you drift away from shore. All blinds must be within 500 yards of shoreline or display an offshore float-

ing blind license, and those occupants who overnight in such blinds must
pay all applicable lodging taxes.

STAMPS

Federal Migratory Stamp

Any duck hunter sixteen or over must purchase a current federal
duck stamp and attach it to his or her license. This stamp must be signed
across the image before use or the special migratory deputies of the U.S.
Post Office will crush all your Christmas cookie boxes from home.

State Migratory Waterfowl Stamp

Most all states require the purchase of a state stamp by both residents and nonresidents. This stamp allows you to shoot waterfowl that
migrate within the state. The good news is that the state doesn't require
you to buy the full-sized print version of politically correct game birds in
flight. Not yet.

Nonresident Featherbearing Waterfowl Stamp

Some states require out-of-state shooters to fund refeathering of
birds not brought to bag.

Nonresident Furbearing Waterfowl Stamp

This stamp will be sold to any nonresident who buys the feather-
bearing stamp.

Waterfowl Restoration Stamp

Some states require nonresident shooters to pay extradition expens-
es for resident waterfowl not brought to bag.

Wildlife Habitat Stamp

Some states require nonresident shooters to pay for the habitat consumed in their pursuit of waterfowl—which can be substantial.

CHAPTER 9

RETRIEVERS

People want retrievers for duck hunting for two very important reasons: in-season retrieving and year-round, quiet, non-judgmental companionship. Since duck hunting and bird retrieval can sometimes swallow only a fifth of the year (which is also the standard swallow in a duck shack), the remaining unproductive months require a companion that will sit motionless while you recount the seemingly endless (even to you) days in the marsh. In this very important selection of the best year-round, all-round hunting partner, full consideration must be given to a pig.

Buck's current hunting pig, Dorothy, comes from a long line of champion retrievers. This regal bloodline of hunting pigs was important enough to be commemorated with the first duck stamp to feature a nonduck subject, to wit, Buck's Queen Duroc, captured in paint by the famous wildlife artist Reese S. Pieces for the 1959–1960 competition. It was said that Buck's Queen couldn't mark but she could run a straight line through the meat packing plants in South St. Paul. This painting of a duck-pig with a dead mallard offended many Labrador owners; under intense pressure and some evidence of financial gain, the judges changed the rules so the only subjects forevermore on federal duck stamps are ducks, live ducks that is. Decoys need not apply. Coots either.

WHY A HUNTING OR DUCK-PIG?

Famous hobby farmer George Orwell described pigs as "generally recognized as being the cleverest of the animals." Compared to other farmyard animals a pig is:

- *not as doltish as a horse.*
- *prettier than a cow.*
- *not as nasty as a goose or gander.*

Compared to other household pets a pig is:

- *not as mean-spirited as a small dog.*
- *not as dishonest as a cat.*
- *not as noisy as a parakeet.*

Disadvantage to using a pig: A pig may eat a downed bird.

Advantage to using a pig (please don't read this part to Dorothy!): You can eat a pig that eats downed birds.

You have no reason to be nervous about a decision to go whole hog. Pigs have been around for forty million years, and man a mere million. Unlike modern man, pigs have had to go through little evolutionary change to get to where they are today. Man claims to have domesticated swine in China as long ago as 5000 B.C. Woman claims to have domesticated waterfowlers as long ago as last minute but we all know better than that.

Hunting pigs have been around for hundreds of years. From the eleventh to the fifteenth century, pigs were used by European commoners forbidden to use hunting dogs. The advantages should be obvious: A pig likes the muddy, wet conditions that define a shooting blind, it will eat leftover cold sandwiches, and it doesn't shed in hotel beds. A properly attended pig exhibits few, if any, "piggy" attributes and easily learns how to retrieve birds, especially those along the shore. A pig is intelligent, loyal, devoted, clean, and caring. It never eats more than what it needs, will drink hard (and cheap) liquor with you, and will keep all your confidences. It will appreciate and return cynical grunts. A porcine retriever is also good for the better half. In the first six months, a duck-pig can provide over four thousand pounds of fertilizer for your spouse's vegetable garden, and unlike a dog, won't stick a nose up her or, for that matter, your gardening skirt.

The larger human family benefits even more by the existence of pigs. Donor pigs give their heart valves and even the skin off their own backs to often unworthy human burn patients. Folk medicine has long recommended pig parts to cure and ward off a long list of ailments. Even Uncle Sam was a porker: In the War of 1812, a provisioner named Sam Wilson supplied pork to the troops and became a symbol of the country's greatness.

GENERAL ORDER OF PIGDOM

The duck-pig has an important place in the large and distinguished natural order. Dorothy is, of course, a mammal like us. Of the order Artiodactyla, she has an even number of toes like us (if we count both feet) and is a suiform to join those of us long at the tooth. Her Suidae family of long-snouted, omnivorous, grunting terrestrials includes the wild boars of Europe, Asia, and India, all domestic pigs, and, for that matter, the wild bores in your blind.

There are two opposing body types in pigdom and all breeds are mixtures of either. The wild European boar is a marbled, muscular pig with an arched back. The Asian-type pig is more docile, with fat layers and a lower back. A mix of both, American pigs are generally more muscular than their English ancestors but then we haven't lost an empire. The most obvious distinguishing trait for most observers is color: white, white belt, black, black spotted, black with white points, and belted.

The National Association of Hunting Hog Retrievers recognizes eight pure breeds:

American Berkshire

A medium-sized retriever named after the county or "shire" of Berks in England where it was found. First of the pig pioneers, the Berkshire arrived stateside in the early 1800s yet with its long history is not as popular as it once was. The Berkie is black with white on its face, feet, and tail tip, has erect ears, a short head, and a short upturned nose on a broad, slightly dished face. Napoleon, the leader of the animal revolt in George Orwell's *Animal Farm,* "was a large, rather fierce-looking" Berkshire boar, the only Berkshire on the farm, "not much of a talker, but with a reputation for getting his own way." It's not clear what his henchmen, Squealer and Snowball, "a cheery little pig," were—probably mutant canines. Comrade Napoleon lead the barnyard revolt hiding behind a typical cryptic inaugural cliché— "All animals are equal. But some animals are more equal than others!"—and created the first animal police state. This boar deserves the distinction of being the first police "pig" and the tale carries an important lesson on campaign promises.

BERKSHIRE

Chester White

An American large light- or white-skinned breed from Chester County, Pennsylvania, with English origins tempered by New York influences. This hardy crossbreeder has a short face, semilopped to lopped floppy ears, and big hams. Wilbur of E. B. White's *Charlotte's Web* was probably a Chester White since he had white hair and was not as trim as a Yorkshire. The most popular Chester White was Arnold Ziffel, costar of CBS-TV's *Green Acres*, who as the more intelligent (and some say prettier) half of the household won the Performing Animal Television Star of the Year Award in 1968 and 1969.

CHESTER WHITE

Duroc

A large, hardy, pinkish red breed named after an American breeder's famous trotter horse. Sprung from the loin chops of the Durocs of New York and the Reds of New Jersey, the former Duroc-Jerseys have a handsome profile and a keen intelligence. Keen of mind, deep of body, and high-arched of back, this very popular breed runs gold to mahogany, with cherry red the prized rind color. This well-marbled, well-mannered, droopy-eared retriever is sometimes raised for lard. Judging from typical duck blind occupants, this pig should be a perfect body fit.

DUROC

Hampshire

An exotic black retriever with a belt of white wrapping its shoulders and forelegs. The black color is less susceptible to sunburn so in early season you

HAMPSHIRE

need only cover or camo the belt. Another expatriate Brit, this active, alert grazer with a snout that points straight out is well known for its lean cuisine. In fact, Hampshire boars have the largest loin eyes of all breeds, which is a good thing for you to know and for them to understand.

American Landrace

The Great Dane of retrievers, this European import is too often found in Danish gift meat packs. The expatriate has large floppy ears attached to a narrow head sitting on a long, lean, white or pink body. Since the Landrance has three more ribs than other retrievers, geneticists have tried to breed a second trailer of its ribs for the barbecue crowd but too many state shipping laws prohibit.

AMERICAN LANDRACE

Poland China

The Poland China was developed in Ohio in the early 1800s and was a top market breed and a very popular lard pig. This cross-breeder is black with white legs, often with splashes of white on the face and on the tip of the tail, has a short snout and droopy long ears, and is known for its high energy. Large boars can top off at a thousand pounds, sows at nine hundred pounds, making for a commanding—no, make that overwhelming—presence at duck-pig field trials.

POLAND CHINA

Spotted Poland China

A mix of the Poland China with Gloucester Old Spotted devel-

SPOTTED POLAND CHINA

oped in central Indiana, this duck-pig has big white spots in unusual shapes that can be effective natural camo. To be truly Spotted, this animal must be 50 percent black and 50 percent white in big spots. Big-boned and stocky, this everyman's retriever pig loves the outdoors and, should the inferior canines fail as they are wont to do, will always bring home the bacon.

Yorkshire

The very popular Yorkie is the only pig that had its picture taken with an American president in the White House (Ike in 1955). Originally from Yorkshire county, this British immigrant arrived on our shores in the late 1800s and quickly became a breeders' favorite with its ability to produce the largest litters. These pink or white sows have a slightly dished face, short snout, and ears that go erect when being mounted, much like their former titled masters, representatives of a less distinguished lineage.

YORKSHIRE

There are, of course, other hunting breeds to consider. One of the oldest breeds, the Tamworth or "Big Red" is a long-nosed English Baron that likes to live outdoors and is colored like an Irish setter. Fortunately, the Tamworth is much brighter than the dog best described as a four-legged, long-haired taro root.

There have been a few famous Minnesota crossbreeds, numbered one to four, the first a mix of a Landrace and an English Tamworth. Buck's hunting pig, Dorothy, is officially recognized around Big Babe Lake as Northernmost Minnesota Number One, a custom hybrid of a Canadian Yorkshire chosen for its sense of humor and fondness for cheap beer, and from Buck's shadowy past in the Far East, a pig from the North Caucasus carrying the color genes for camouflage. There are noticeable trace behavioral elements from an unusual encounter with a gray wolf up north where the U.S. Park Service is raising canines for the Yellowstone National Wolf Petting Park.

DUCK-DOGS

If you still lack the courage to "buck" the bloated dog lobby, be aware that you have been bamboozled by the best. Admittedly, it does seem that dogs have been around for a long time, but that is more a function of their fawning nature. Artists have often used dogs as an expression of the simpler world, but Eduard Manet and Pierre-Auguste Renoir did dog portraits only to pay the candlelight bills. Charles Dickens, Samuel Johnson, Lewis Carroll, and Edward Lear generously crafted verse for the more literate pig owners.

Given the emotional relationship between canines and their owners, the dog has unfortunately become a surrogate human being, listening for "his master's voice." It's not clear who first said a dog is man's best friend but it must have been someone who owned an obedience school. Dogs are man's best friend because man can be the master and can take great pleasure in making a fool of himself, which you don't need to do with a pig.

If you still insist on using a dog instead of an eager and able pig, Buck will review your breed choices at no extra charge but *remember:* Ogsday Reay Otnay Otay Ebay Ruffledtay Ithway (Dogs are not to be truffled with)!

Buck estimates that there are about two million hunting retrievers in the United States. The major American hunting breeds are the Chesapeake Bay retriever, the American water spaniel, and the black-and-tan coonhound, all three part of the great American melting pot. The first, the more common water dog, is a cross between a Newfoundland and perhaps a black-and-tan coonhound; the second is a cross between other spaniel and retriever breeds; and the third and oldest breed is thought to have evolved from several English hounds, including the bloodhound, with a dash of American foxhound.

Chesapeake Bay Retriever

Bred bigger and tougher to bring back unimaginable market limits in unmanageable big bay conditions, Chesapeakes specialize in retrieving wounded, angry old birds backstroking across big water. Unlike many shooters, a Chessie can mark several birds at a time. Their origin is colorful: The breed was thought to have originated from two Newfoundland pups rescued from an English brig full of codfish that ran aground off the coast of Maryland in 1807. Chesapeakes can be possessive and self-reliant and have a reputation for being pig-headed which, in Buck's book, is an attribute. In fact, only the Chessie approaches the personal integrity of a pig, and in the real world is the only logical substitute for a hunting boar. The state dog of Maryland, these independent swamp collies are often as surly as their original watermen owners.

American Water Spaniel

The state dog of Wisconsin was originally lured to the area by promises of cheap beer and sausages. This curly-headed midwesterner settled and developed near Osh Kosh. Purists, of course, fret about whether this water dog should be classified as a retriever or a flushing spaniel. Built more like a springer, this smaller, long-tailed dog has a retriever's double coat, which makes some purists think impure thoughts. The American water spaniel may mature and learn slower than the Labrador but this breed can be taught to grin and yodel which, b'gosh, is pretty darn important in Wisconsin.

Black-and-Tan Coonhound

Originally bred to hunt up and tree raccoons and possums, the coonhound is best used to retrieve tree-dwelling ducks such as the wood duck, fulvous tree duck, and the more rare black-bellied tree duck of south Texas trying to crawl back up to safety. Once the coonhound has the scent of a wronged wood duck, this bloodhound won't give up. Affectionate, attentive, and with a great voice, the black-and-tan is officially recognized by both the American and Canadian Kennel Clubs which, to someone who eats a lot of raccoons and possums, means *absolutely nothing!*

Foreigners

Beagle

Porky Pig's hunting dog, a beagle, unfortunately tried to bring Daffy Duck to bag but was flattened by that "crazy darn fool duck!" Once that happens, a beagle loses its edge. Speaking of dogs that have lost their edge, the most famous beagle, of course, stopped chasing the Red Baron along post-W.W.I flyways once he discovered that appearing on the airwaves for a major insurance company pays much better.

Cocker Spaniel

This is the original "cocking" or woodcock hunting dog; the taller, heavier English cocker spaniel was originally bred for field hunting. In fact, the dukes of Marlborough championed cockers until they too died of emphysema and other unfiltered disorders. Unfortunately, today both the English and American cocker fashion breeders have concentrated on the looks of the dog, leaving the half-cocked show qualities in and fully cocked field qualities out. If you mix the intelligence of the typical cocker breeder with the tireless enthusiasm of the breed, you'll end up with a dog that will run as fast as it can toward some point on the distant horizon. Today's show cockers are best used around the house, outfitted (or rather in-fitted) with a broom handle and sprayed with Endust.

Dachshund

From much larger German ancestors, these four-legged bratwursts were originally bred to crawl into holes after badgers or "dachs." The big forelegs on these Schultze's don't hold the deep breast high enough off the sharp marsh grasses so from personal experience, Buck recommends a protective chest pad. The smooth-haired, black-and-tan-dappled miniature makes a fine retriever and a hunting companion that, with a little reassurance, loves to ride in the game pocket of a hunting jacket. These national dogs of Germany have a keen sense of smell and are renowned for their ability to find a wounded bird, which makes them perfect for the age of steel shot.

Golden Retriever

Once thought to be descendants of a band of Russian circus dogs, the golden is a mix and remix of yellow, black, and liver-colored flat-coated retrievers and tweed water spaniels, with Irish setter thrown in for color, a bloodhound for tracking, and—not often discussed in breeder circles—a large hamster for its preference to live indoors. CAT scans on golden retrievers may come up negative but that is no reason to assume they are brain-dead. They may just be asleep or tired. A sample of the golden's diminished awareness: A golden will let an owner comb the burrs from its long, curly coat without much fuss. A sample of the golden owner's diminished awareness: An owner will spend the afternoon combing burrs out of the dog's long hairs while short-haired buddies will be in the tavern watching the football game.

Irish Water Spaniel

Largest of the spaniel family, this endurance swimmer was bred for retrieving. The Irish water spaniel is smart but best trained by a family member. Some perform naturally with a minimum of formal training, others are tougher to train. Like its early masters, this hard-headed loyalist will pick a fight with another Irish spaniel over a single helping of corned beef and cabbage. As the English have learned, all Irish breeds should be coaxed, not forced, into doing anything.

Labrador Retriever
The very popular Labrador is smart, willing to learn, eager to please, and has a long history of service. As described by Richard A. Wolters in his fine book *Retriever*, "The St. Hubert's dog was brought by Devon woodsmen to Newfoundland for hunting and once the fishermen used them to fetch loose fish that floated free of the hooks and nets." The most direct descendants of this original line of retrievers still have fishy-smelling breath and this lineage may account for the high Lab glee while rolling in dead fish. Labradors are a good choice for a combo retriever package: a dog for major offshore work and a pig for the more important onshore work. A Labrador's intelligence comes closest to a pig's and the dog can be described as almost being as handsome as a pig. While there is a fashion to downsize this breed for obscure and ultimately meaningless competitions, a large-boned Labrador, especially one from a northern climate and weighing nearly one hundred pounds, is hard to beat. Literally. Three designer colors are recognized as official yet the original yellow color (actually a rich gold) is the cooler color. Buck's first Labrador, Pearl, was off-white in color and had impeccable manners. On the few occasions she veered near a duck hunt, she avoided the battlefield yet never failed to be interested in all the after-hunt activity.

BUCK'S SPECIAL NOTE: Male black Labradors are prone to having just awful intestinal distress. On the way to some sporting adventure, an older brother's black Labrador actually smiled while cutting the cheese in the backseat. Then again, he might have gotten into the snack foods we had up front.

If you still insist on having a retriever dog rather than a fine hunting pig, at least reconsider your specific needs. Retrieving takes up a few minutes of your hunting time, but guarding your gear, not to mention your downed birds, from in-laws and other rascals is another matter altogether. If security is a problem, select a guard dog, either to stay in the blind with you or to send out as a long-toothed escort for your hunting pig.

Guard Dogs

Pit Bull

These handsome rascals are either ferociously loyal or loyally ferocious. With the same disposition as a goose pit boss, these tenacious terriers are not welcome in many neighborhoods, but goose pit bosses don't make good neighbors either. The pit bull is the perfect companion for the hunter who likes to hunt and most likely lives alone, and is the best retriever for the alligator-infested waters of the deep South.

Poodle

Actually bred to be a European water retriever, the dog is called a *Pudel* in Germany and the local slang word *pudelin* means "splashing about in the water." In France, a poodle is called *caniche* and American tourists are called much worse. When these aristocratic dogs were introduced to the decadent French, hairdressers to the waterfowlers clipped the top of the retrievers' heads in the shape of a decoy.

The full standard-sized poodle has a long, distinguished hunting heritage. Posting a nicely coifed guard poodle by your blind will keep most hunters away. At least most resident hunters.

Rottweiler

A very popular guard dog, the rottweiler was originally used as a dri-ving dog and then left behind by the Romans for the two-legged burghers of Rottweil, Germany, to herd their four-legged burgers-to-be to market. The hard-working black dogs with tan markings are now seeing service with foreign police forces. Waterfowl refuge managers with sunrise mob control needs have been spotted talking to rottweiler breeders in hopes of taking a bite out of crime.

ONE MORE REASON TO OWN A PIG RATHER THAN A DOG

You can't teach an old dog new tricks. Or was it a new dog old tricks? Your choice.

CHAPTER 10

BUYING AND TRAINING YOUR BOG HOG

To market, to market, to buy a duck-pig
Home again, home again, dancing a jig
Riding to market to buy a duck-pig
Home again, home again, jiggedy jig.

To buy a good pig, you should know the language of the trade:

Shoat: An immature pig.

Wiener: A shoat weighing twenty-five to forty pounds.

Hog: A big, purebred pig weighing 100 to 120 pounds.

Boar: A breeding male.

Sow: A breeding female that has produced one litter.

Gilt: An unbred, litterless female.

Barrow: A very young male shoat stripped of manhood.

Rig: A partially castrated male (one testicle mistakenly left inside).

Stag: A male castrated at a mature breeding age.

You'll want to find a pig with a good nose, a pig that can smell well (not necessarily good) and also interpret those smells. In Celtic legend, Merlin often had a farmyard pig at his side and it was the pig, with its terrific smeller, that found the Holy Grail, the mythical cup of Jesus at the Last Supper. Even Lancelot couldn't best the ordinary farm pig. The French *chercheuse* sow has a nose good for at least five years, ferreting black truffles from under oak tree roots. Popular folklore holds that pigs can not only smell but see the wind and predict storms for good sports who don't have enough sense to come in out of the rain.

Look for a pig that wants to work as hard as you do. If you don't hunt that hard, that pig won't be hard to find. There is good reason to pick a pig that looks like its marbled and a-little-oversized new owner—the more muscular the animal, the more extreme its reaction to porcine stress. Don't be concerned with trait identification such as dominance versus subordinance, temperance versus incontinence, and other such canine nonsense.

Buy from a reputable dealer. *Don't buy a pig in a poke!* Unscrupulous middle-aged merchants may still substitute a cat for a pig and as an honest consumer, it's your responsibility to let it out of the bag. Take your time and pick an obviously healthy animal. Feel for hernias. Pull its tail; a good tail is important for training. Pigs are weaned at four weeks and sold at eight weeks, weighing roughly thirty to forty pounds. Don't overlook "small and weak" runts. Fern didn't and Wilbur grew up to be a prize winner. How much to pay? One tradition is to pay one-half the cost of a hundred-pound pig plus $1. Buck has never paid over $50 for a young duck-pig.

Which sex makes the best retriever? Boars are more aggressive. Sows have gentler dispositions and maternal qualities that spill over into sporting attributes. A problem with sows that have had any media exposure is their susceptibility to flattery. Fawning attention on her "moi-ship" will induce ego problems and a little miss piggy will demand superstar status. Buck prefers to train sows because he has had enough training bores.

BUCK'S SPECIAL RETRIEVER PIG TIP: Many prefer to buy a spring shoat; if you decide to purchase a piglet in the fall, you won't be discouraged by its youth. As Winnie-the-Pooh quickly learned, Piglet proved to be an excellent hunting and tracking partner during woozle season.

BUCK'S SPECIAL RETRIEVER PIG TIP REVISITED: If you decide to buy a dog in the fall, you will be discouraged by its youth. Not long ago, Buck was hunting the Susitna Flats near Anchorage. On the first morning, a hunting buddy's young black Labrador bolted out the door of the duck shack and lifted every duck off Stump Lake before we could get our boots on—an action almost as bright as leaving the groceries in the trunk of the car at the float plane dock.

Another advantage of owning and training a duck-pig is that you don't have to worry about all the meaningless canine affectations. There is no pig pedigree, such as AFC, NFC, NFL, ETC, or LTD, to be concerned with. You don't have to pay a fee to a national registry that exists to run lucrative beauty contests and you don't have to pay a fee to Buck (unless you have an extra Jackson in your wallet) for guiding thoughts on pig conformations.

The Original Standard For the Retriever Pig
(Abridged Version)
The American Sty Club

General Appearance

The retriever pig is a strong, handsome, medium-sized animal possessing an all-American conformation that enables it to function as a retrieving retriever pig, the substance and soundness to hunt waterfowl under conditions best described as other-worldly, the character and good sense to avoid the show ring and all the half- and inbreeds therein, and the temperament to be a close personal friend. Physically and mentally, the retriever pig is bred to perform or at least go through the motions of all the required functions in the field and still have time and energy left to wallow around a bit. The most distinguishing characteristics of the retriever pig are its short, sparse, weather-sensitive coat, a nicely twisted tail, a well-shaped head with a broad-backed skull, a dramatic slope to a nose that can best be described as perfect, and its "knowing" friendly eyes, expressing self-esteem and self-knowledge. Above all, the retriever pig must be more psychologically balanced than its hunting partner, enabling it to move in a businesslike manner even when the environment is mayhem. The typical retriever pig is stylish without being *au couture*, a solid citizen without haughtiness. The retriever pig is bred primarily as a working retriever pig.

Size

The height and length of a retriever pig can be most anything. Any variance greater than one-half inch above and below is cause for celebration. Approximate weight in first fall peak working condition in males is 120 pounds and in females, 100 pounds.

Proportion

The length from the point of the shoulder where the loins merge with the tender picnic hams to where the tenderloins end in rump roasts should be equal to or slightly longer than the distance from Mr. Dithers's withers to the ground. Distance from the top of the ham hocks to knuckles that deserve pickling should be half the square root (converted to inches) of the IQ of miniature-pig breeders plus twenty or so. The body should be of sufficient length to allow for a straight, efficient stride but the pig shouldn't appear unpiglike in outline.

Substance

The substance or warp and woof and bone structure should be proportionate. Slim, designer models raised for meat are as inappropriate as a pig raised just for lard. Retriever pigs shall be worked to a well-muscled condition yet wrapped in a nice layer of marbled fat for taste.

Head and Skull

The skull should be beautifully well developed with necessary exaggeration. The brow should slope beautifully toward a nose, draping powerful jaws with overbite allowed.

Nose

The nose should be rounded, with a nice flat surface at the end, and with two well-rounded nostrils. When clean, the nose should be a healthy pink.

Teeth

A pig's teeth should be kept out of sight.

Ears

Ears can be floppy or erect according to breed; each is prettier than a silk purse, and both are better to hear you with.

Eyes

Piercing, alert eyes showing a knowing nature are a trademark of pigs in general. Eye color should be humanlike.

Neck

The neck should be long enough for the pig to root and retrieve game.

Topline

The back is slightly rounded or bowed, indicating fully developed tenderloins.

Body

The retriever pig should show on its long flanks the musculature that houses some of the better breakfast meats.

Forequarters

Forequarters should be muscular, and in balance with and connected to the hindquarters.

Shoulders

The picnic shoulders should drape the large tasty hocks above the front feet.

Front Legs

When viewed from the front, the front legs should seem straight yet noticeably shorter than the back legs, giving them a particularly fine road-hugging look.

Hindquarters

The retriever pig's hindquarters are muscular and well developed from the base of the tail through the hams down to the hind feet. The legs are strongly boned and broad with moderate angulation at the stifle and powerful hams. A little marbling is not bad either. The rear toes are cloven. Hind feet that are not good eating when pickled are serious defects and are to be faulted.

Coat

The absence of a coat is a distinctive feature of the retriever pig. A coat is just not important. Any alteration of the natural bristle should be severely penalized. Retriever pigs can suffer the heartbreak of psoriasis if not properly loved.

Color

Retriever pig colors are white, red, black, and any shades thereof. Spots and stripes appropriate to the breed are rather expected. Dark spots not characteristic of a breed may be just dirt, which is okay. White hairs from aging or scarring are hard to distinguish from the normal bristles and that is okay too.

Movement

All movements of the retriever pig should be effortless, much like its intestinal movements. When you watch a retriever pig approach, its legs should form straight lines with only a little bowleggedness. If you look from behind, and after feeding farther behind is best, the hind legs should seem to move in a parallel plane with the front legs, unless the animal is sitting down. The hocks should smoothly carry the weight and, when smoked, taste great. When viewed from the side, the tenderloins, spare ribs, hams, and slabs of bacon should all move effortlessly. Movement faults (obliquely referred to above) interfering with performance in the field have more to do with a bad diet than with weaving or paddling, whatever paddling is.

Temperament

True retriever pig temperament is as much a trademark of the breeds as the curly tail. The ideal retriever pig disposition is one of worldly intelligence, a mature respect for others, and a heartfelt desire to engage in a long-term relationship. The retriever pig is a gentle friend and go-boom companion. Human aggressiveness toward retriever pigs should be severely penalized.

DISQUALIFICATIONS

1. Any physical resemblance to the unfortunate designer miniature pigs.

2. A too-clean nose.

3. Two too-clean eyes.

4. Untwisting or other altering of the finely twisted tail.

5. Any color change except for the temporary use of hunter camouflage pigments.

It's important that a retriever pig be in good health and a physical by a licensed swinologist is recommended. Test youngsters for roundworm. Many piggers vaccinate against swine erysipelas, a skin disease. If the needle teeth of the baby pig haven't been clipped, do so with an electrician's wire cutters. At six weeks, all males or boars should be castrated, which is actually not a bad idea for the other bores in the blind.

Feed manufacturers recommend only their own brand of market mix, with prices inflated to pay the costs of expensive market segmentation. Retriever pigs are less fussy about their dining. All that's needed is a balanced dry pig food and a good clean water source. In the early training, a supply of apples or pears is helpful. Pigs won't naturally overeat or "pig out," they'll eat just enough.

BRINGING YOUR NEW RETRIEVER HOME
Use either a dog carrier or a gunnysack if a short distance. If you are traveling a long distance, it may be worthwhile to sedate the young one.

The Retriever's New Home
Your new pig has few physical requirements: a warm, safe, comfortable place to sleep, a place to eat and root, and a place to go to the bathroom. If you feel a need to start the retriever in the house, note that another famous pig grew out of his box near the stove in the kitchen. Fern kept moving Wilbur; when he outgrew the bigger box in the wood-

shed, she moved him to a large wooden box full of straw under an apple tree. The housing need not be complicated: Piglet lived in the middle of a beech tree.

After huffing and puffing through two experiments in construction that didn't hold up, Buck finally built a brick home for Dorothy.

Pigs have a long and not-repressed memory of shelters made of sticks and straw that make the hairs on their chin- ny-chin-chin stand on end. Dorothy's original homestead was built with custom bricks of a mixture of Mississippi mud and marsh grasses from one of Buck's per- sonal blinds. Along with her new brick home, Dorothy enjoys a yard with enough pasture for rooting valuable minerals and nutrients, "a nice apple tree," and "a nice field of turnips" nearby.

CONDITIONING AND TRAINING YOUR DUCK-PIG

It takes a good three to four months to get a pig in shape for the season. A program of moderate exercise will build the hams and condition the heart and lungs. A pig isn't a pack animal like a dog. Train one pig at a time. You'll only have to show the pig once and he or she will get it. Once you get into the spirit of training, you won't remember ever hav- ing as much fun since the dogs ate your little sister.

Conditioning

Start your training workouts at ten minutes a day and build to eleven minutes. Go slow. If your pig is tired, his or her tail will not wiggle like it should. Your new retriever may decide to lie down. That's a good time for you to lie down, too.

In the heat of the summer, keep your duck-pig cool. Pigs don't per- spire like the canine sweat hogs so on hot days, watch for heavy breathing, bright gums, and general signs of exhaustion. If it's too hot, stop doing what you're doing and share a cool malt beverage with your little buddy.

When training a duck-pig, always remember:

1. The pig may be as smart as you but it doesn't hurt to repeat a request. A pig wants you to succeed first as a person then as a duck hunter.

2. Don't whisper. Pigs prefer a loud boisterous call.

3. The pig likes consistency but not so much straight stuff that a little helter-skelter wouldn't be entertaining.

4. The pig respects you and maintaining this respect requires mutual respect. You may be the boss in your house, but let the pig be the lord or lordette of its own manner.

5. The pig's needs are directly tied to comfort: comfort food, clean water, and an outdoor toilet.

Training pigs is very different from training the lesser canines. Throw away any force or natural systems. The philosophy of using praise to train and then withdrawing praise as the work becomes a reward in itself doesn't compute. A pig doesn't need your praise.

Never give a command to a pig that it can't accomplish, such as "jump" or "bark like a dog." If you feel the need, release your little pal from one request by using another request but—unlike owners of golden retrievers—never apologize for a wrong request. Pigs will respond favorably to multiple requests such as "eat" then "eat more" or "wallow" and "wallow more." Let sleeping hogs lie! If your retriever isn't taking lessons as expected, stop and start up tomorrow. Or the next day. *Every hog has its day!*

Sample Requests

"Come"

Squat and call the pig by its name (it helps if you have an apple or pear in your hand). If you put a noose on its nose and try to long-leash it into the proper response, you will lose a good friend in the process.

BUCK'S SPECIAL TIP: Pigs have comfort zones. The five- to six-foot distant security blanket is the first obstacle you'll have to overcome.

"Sit"

Pull up on leashed collar and push butt down while you request. It helps if you have an apple or pear in its mouth and often that still isn't enough. What do you need a pig to sit for anyway? If it does sit for you, give yourself lots of praise and both of you a fine malt beverage. It is a minor miracle.

"Kennel" or "Kennel Up"

If you must use this request, go into the sty first and try to bribe your retriever in. Some handlers push a reluctant retriever pig. Much less successful handlers will try to back a pig into a preferred location, sometimes with a pail over its head. You might as well put the pail over your head for such a foolish notion.

"Whoa" or alternative, "Help!"

Use this request when the apple or pear in your hand has disappeared into a frothy smile.

"Stay" or the more popular alternative, "Give Me Time To Move"

Give this request while holding or filling a food container. If the request is used just to make the pig stay away from you when all it wants to do is be close, shame on you!

"Heel"

This request is easy to teach as pigs enjoy chewing on your heel or for that matter any part of your shoe. A right-handed shooter should have his retriever chew on the left heel, a left-handed shooter on the right heel. A pig may want to go ahead of you and a handheld plywood board or hurdle or a rope around the back leg may be just enough restraint.

"Fetch"

Start retrieving as play. Throw an apple down the hallway. Say "fetch" as your pal moves to eat the fruit and feel good that it seems that the command is working. Next throw a duck carcass stuffed with apples, then a duck carcass without apples. The pig will not like the plain duck and may bring it back for stuffing. At that point, you are in a win-win situation. Enjoy it while it lasts.

"Wallow"

No instructions needed.

Sometimes all requests may be for naught and a general call that implies well-being and a happy home may be needed. Competition calling at the Stutter and Phart World Championships includes contestants from all around the country using mouth calls like "soooo . . . oeyyy," "whooooeeyyyy," or simply "peeeeeeeeeeeeeeeeeeg!" The master word or general hail call "to known" to bring pork chops leaping from their plates" was described by the great pig lover P. G. Wodehouse in his story "Pig-hoo-o-o-o-ey": "You'll want to begin the hoo' in a low minor of two quarter notes in four-four time. From this build gradually to a higher note, until at last the voice is soaring in full crescendo, reaching F sharp on the natural scale and dwelling for two retarded half-notes, then breaking into a shower of accidental grace-notes."

BUCK'S SPECIAL TRAINING TIP: If you are training a piglet who is unlikely to have been born with a silver spoonerism in its mouth, spleak painly!

Once the calls and requests seem, at least to you, common knowledge, it's time to start conditioning for noise but *not* by shouting at the pig when it has goofed up. Clap your hands then start making louder noises when feeding your pet. Associating good things like eating with loud noises prevents gun shyness. Successful trainers take their young shoat into the field, throw an apple with one hand, and shoot off a smaller then larger gun with the other. Remember: Gun shyness is created by the owner.

Pigs do not need too sharp a focus in any of their training! Slowly introduce your retriever to large water and not too cold a water at that. Some trainers teach the pig to carry a stick in its mouth before taking it on a leash into the water so it doesn't paddle, as inferior canines are wont to do. Most good owners also trim their duck-pig's hooves so it can't cut its throat when swimming.

Take any pig to a boat with caution. Most pigs do not like unsteady surfaces and are only in your duck boat out of blind trust. Little Pig Robinson took much too easily to a big boat ride, another example of out-of-control artistic license.

Teaching the Pig To Point

The principal advantage to owning a duck-pig is that it may point toward a downed bird. How do you know when it's pointing? In the Northern Hemisphere, the tail curl twists counterclockwise, in the Southern, clockwise; when pointing, the tail will unwrap in the opposite direction. Buck often likes to hunt Dorothy in tandem with his old yellow Labrador, Pearl. Note that in the lineup, it is not necessary to cast Pearl before swine.

Teaching the Pig To Retrieve

It's possible and depends on your moral strength and sportsman's ethic. If you're a lout, an overshooter, or a poacher who uses silent or verbal directional casts, none of this will work. Duck-pigs will surprise only the true waterfowler.

PROBLEM PIGS

On the rare occasion when the retriever is a dominant or alpha pig, it may need a little special discipline. If a pig challenges you for either space or food, squeeze the back of its neck. When an adult pig tries to challenge, some handlers will stand and try to stare the bully down, but Buck prefers to sit on its back.

BUCK'S SPECIAL TRAINING TIP: Whatever you do, don't put an electronic collar on your pig. You do not want an electric pig! Force-training has no place in Buck's world.

If an adult pig still doesn't behave like a good pig, it's time to pull out the most important piece of discipline you have:

YOUR REWARD FOR TAKING GREAT
CARE IN THE PURCHASE AND TRAINING!

CHAPTER 11

PREPARING FOR THE HUNT

Duck hunters need a place to hunt. The lucky ones get to hunt in their own backyard. They are called residents. Everyone else is called a nonresident. You can be a nonresident in your own state, especially if you are from a big city.

Nonresident duck hunters have several choices in selecting a place to hunt. They can call a famous duck hunting camp like Buck's Duck Hunting Lodge and arrange for a full-bore, Dead Duck Society guided expedition. Nonresidents can also book an independent guide service and stay in a nearby town or decide to do it all on their own, hunting public land for a no-frills, no-kills weekend.

The principal advantages of the first two choices are that resident guide services know where the birds are, have the right equipment, and are likely to have all the good habitat locked up in lease. The principal advantage of the last option is that it is cheaper.

Once all the arrangements have been made, it won't be long

WATERFOWL REDUCTION AREA

•OPEN•
TO HUNTING

BY FISH AND WILDLIFE SERVICE
EMPLOYEES & THEIR FAMILIES

before it's time to head to the coast, the east side, the west side, over the mountains and through the woods. The most important thing to remember as a nonresident and/or big-city person is that you are an unofficial ambassador to foreign lands chock full of locals who talk and act funny, foodstuffs that look and taste funny, and customs that are quaint and possibly harmful. Quite likely you are the city feller Ed Zern described who "thinks any person that wears the same shirt two days in a row is picturesque." The U.S. State Department is responsible for issuing travel advisories to city folks leaving the country so Buck feels sorta responsible for issuing the following advisories to those entering the country.

LODGING

If you are not staying at a lodge, you will stay at a local establishment and your guide will meet you in the morning at some local café or truck stop. When you first pull into town, most of your hunting party must go directly to the police station or sheriff's office (as required by their parole warden to be warned yet again to avoid a life of crime) and have their weapons re-welded in a three-shot configuration.

Your accommodation choices are bed and breakfasts (B&Bs), motels, or hotels. B&Bs are old houses where owners called proprietors jealously guard their pet ducks on the pond out back. Motels are made of either wood or concrete blocks. For your hunting party, it's better if the motel is made of concrete blocks. Hotels are motels of more than two stories but if you send ol' Buck a Jackson he'll tell you more than two good motel stories. When you check into your lodging, front desk clerks will place your hunting party in rooms as far from normal people as possible, yet near the ice machine and mix dispenser. There may be signs saying NO DOGS IN THE ROOM or NO DOGS ON THE BEDS but there will be no signs about your duck-pig, another reason to go whole hog.

Once the gear is stashed and you've selected a bed far from those with late-night breathing problems, most nonresidents like to see the sights a little before it gets dark, top off the gas in the ol' buckmobile, and head down to the local tavern to pound down a few brewskis and burgers before turning in.

Nonresident Alert

Local taverns are, at best, demilitarized zones and, at worst, free-fire zones. You'll know you are in the wrong place when:

the local louts standing at the end of the bar who are drinking shooters out of eight-ounce shot glasses start grumbling about out-of-towners who shoot all the birds.

the local louts standing wherever they please with empty eight-ounce shot glasses and still grumbling about out-of-towners who shoot all the birds take all the booths, stools, and tables including yours.

Nonresidents should only frequent local bars where the incest doesn't go back more than two generations. In these commercial hotel or club adult beverage operations, duck hunters can practice their waterfowling skills.

HOW TO DECOY LOCAL HENS ON THE LOCAL FLYWAYS

Successful hunters first select their camo to carefully match the country-western, sports, or disco habitat. Next, to set up a proper blind, place your decoys on an established flight pattern. Resident flyways are always anchored by the lady's bathroom and local hens make two or three flights a night along this path. This is where an ol' Alaskan skybuster friend of Buck's sets up his blind and decoys within calling range for pass-shooting; jump-shooting around the bar or near the dance floor is not nearly as successful. Few techniques work well when there is lots of space to land in heavily hunted habitat such as big airport hotels during Superbowl weekends. Resident hens are cautious and not known to decoy well. They gather in tight little flocks and don't pay much attention to migratory drakes.

Set your drink decoys in front of two empty chairs on the side of the blind facing the evening flight. Until they see the decoys, other hunters might try to take the empty chairs. Early in the evening flight, species identification is important, with points given for the greater of the species and bonus for large redheads. Begin calling with the hail, "Do you need a place to land?" followed with quick chatter and one-liners. If the birds are just circling, the "come on back" call is used. If the callers see a pair of less desirable hens approaching the set, they pull the deeks closer to the blind, forcing old or ugly coots to flare. If a hen in full plumage suddenly lands and the caller is not ready, all he will see is tail feathers. If a hen falls rather than lands, she may be suffering from intestinal poisoning and/or parasites and it may be time to call the wardens guarding the door. If you don't lead hens properly, you may just break a wing and if they do land, give them your very best shot. Heed the ol' skybuster's advice: Not all hens get prettier at closing time, but enough do!

THE ALARM

The most important decision of duck hunting the night before the hunt is not who picks up the check (even though that may be the priciest), it's what time the alarm clock should be set for. Once this matter is settled, the second most important question is how many alarm clocks should be set. It's unlikely that in your motel there are any operator-assisted wake-up calls. Even the motel owner left town after watching your hunting party check in. The television is unlikely to have a clock but if it does, it is permanently set for the short midday liaisons of the city fathers. The seasoned hunter brings a dependable wind-up alarm clock, a city hunter a digital clock, the junior executive a digital watch, and the senior executive will have his or her secretary call or knock on the door.

The hour set should allow enough time for you to:

> brush your teeth.
>
> get dressed.
>
> grab gear.
>
> go out door.

The hour set should allow enough time for your city buddies to:

> brush, floss, and gargle.
>
> shower and talcum.
>
> apply deodorant.
>
> lather, shave, and apply woodsy cologne.
>
> layer clothing "system" starting with pantyhose and shooting girdle.
>
> clean shooting glasses.

study flyway map.

review Babe's waterfowl identification chart.

polish brass on shells.

apply linseed oil to gun stock.

So What Time Should the Alarm Clock Be Set For?

It really doesn't make much difference. Most waterfowlers sleep so lightly before an early-morning hunt that a clock often doesn't have a chance to go off. When everyone starts moving about, the early morning is often a conflict of needs: the need to eat breakfast and the need to go hunting. Sometimes the first need will alter the second if the diner is serving green eggs and ham. The alteration and any resulting altercations will happen somewhere on the way to the blind.

CHAPTER 12

BLIND BEHAVIOR

ON THE WAY TO THE BLIND

Since shooting hours start early, it's important to put your imitation ducks out so they can be seen in the dawn's early light. Once your rig is parked out of sight, you'll have to either walk or take a boat to your blind with all the gear. Caution must be exercised in the transport of your weapon, especially if you've convinced your ring-wearer to be your gun-bearer, a difficult task in these more liberated times. Unload it!

The early-morning walk or ride will be dark and even though you'll have a flashlight, you won't be able to see all the things that go bump in the night. If you are hunting where there are snakes, alligators, or man-eating catfish, have either the guide or the most junior member lead the way. Around Big Babe Lake, the biggest surprise is muskrat holes or runs.

The danger in going in over your waders is that your wrinkled, fat-lined skin will only protect you in cold water for few minutes. An extended  dip will dangerously lower your body temperature and cool critical internal organs such as your liver. Clogged with the jetsam and flotsam of years of waterfowling, this overworked filter may need replacement and the camp doctor does *not* recommend any donors from your blind. Another danger in going in over your waders in extremely cold water is that a male duck hunter's cajones will hastily retreat in a most northerly direction, not to drop until a promise is made never to do that again. Back up and find a better route!

HOW TO PUT OUT YOUR DECOYS

If you are in a boat, decoys can be dropped over the side. If your blind is on shore, decoys can be thrown or carried out by the person wearing the tallest set of waders. A thrown decoy can land wrong side up, which is good reason for a tall set of legs to wear waders. If the tall set of waders cannot carry all the decoys, you may have to throw the rest. It is a source of no small amusement to lob the imitation ducks so they land or rather splash just out of reach. At least once.

Buck has three basic decoy spread patterns, all variations on a familiar theme and each developed to fit a specific flyway. On Big Babe Lake, the decoys are arranged in an original "pipe" pattern, so named for the pipes market hunters stoked after they shot the first hundred mallards of the day. His patented "cornhusker" pattern works good down through the corn belt along the Mississippi Flyway.

Buck is such a believer in regional adaptations that in cornhusker country, he hunts out of his patented magnum bait blind.

On the Atlantic Flyway, old-timers prefer a more traditional pipe pattern (A) on both large and small waters.

Depending where you hunt on the Central or Pacific Flyway, your choice of patterns may be the more rural corncob or the Eastern Shore duck club pipe. In California and certain parts of the always-high Rockies, another pipe pattern (B) is used:

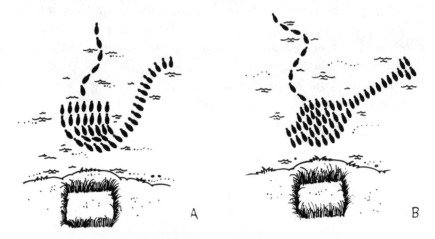

A   B

In the more politically correct refuges, the pattern contains an implicit warning:

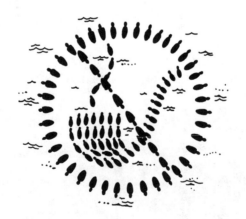

HOW TO ENTER A BLIND

The opening to the blind is usually the back or side door. This does not mean this is the opening an anxious retriever will use. Buck uses a series of special passwords to pass through the doors of the best blinds on Big Babe Lake and will send them to any reader with an extra Jackson in their billfold.

GETTING SETTLED IN THE BLIND

Arrangement of Hunters

If the left is anchored with a left-handed shooter and the right with a strong right-handed shooter and all the rest are nicely placed according to comfort, why does the one with the weakest bladder get the position farthest from the door? Just a question, but a good question. The answer for Buck is to hunt alone. Alone with Dorothy, that is.

Arrangement of Gear

Hunters should have their own seat, whether it be a lard bucket, an ammo box, or a souvenir of last night's activity like a broken bar stool. Certain retrievers should have a nice piece of carpet to sit on. Thermos, lunch, shells, and other errata are cached inside the seats or tucked out of sight in the blind.

Arrangement of Retrievers

Dorothy, Buck's hunting pig, will lie or sit wherever she thinks is right. And that's usually to Buck's left. Which is a slight inconvenience for a left-handed shooter but it's the sort of accommodation you make for a good hunting pal.

FINAL PREPARATIONS

Good hunters look around the blind and hide all shiny objects like shot shell boxes, gun cases, and nonresident hunter orange stocking caps. If it looks like a bright, sunny day is in the works, Buck will check to see if Dorothy wants to wear her camo hunting cap. There still may be time for the last cup of coffee. When the eastern sky lightens, it's almost time, in Nash Buckingham's words, to let the "iron dogs bark."

CHAPTER 13

HOW, WHEN, AND
WHAT TO SHOOT

SHOOTING ETIQUETTE

Nash's daddy told him never to put more shells in his pump gun than his partner can use. If a partner is shooting a double, a good sport won't load but two shells in the gun. If a partner can only hit with one of the two barrels, a good sport won't load but one shell in the gun. If a partner can't hit with either of the barrels, good sport will be had by none. Once your gun is loaded, with safety on, and placed in a safe, easy-to-reach position, reconfirm the firing zones with your hunting partners. In most blinds, the worst shooter usually takes the middle position and partners pick up the extreme left and right.

In a two-man boat, the worst shot usually takes the end closest to the ducks. A three-man boat just tips over.

Guests in Buck's command blinds are assigned positions according to their general sportsmanship and not for the rumored baksheesh. Magnum

drake mallards are easily pulled in by Buck's Bawdy Duck® set and shooting is at slow-flying birds with their landing gear locked in place. Whether
from the right or left, Buck has nonresidents stand and shoot according to
the direction of flight. The closest one standing shoots then sits down;
second shooter stands, shoots, sits; third stands, shoots, sits. If the duck
wants to see where all the noise came from, a reverse shooting order
applies and the reason why Buck and Dorothy prefer to hunt alone
becomes crystal clear!

SHOOTING TECHNIQUE
Blowing holes in the sky is an art and a science complicated by many
variables: hunting conditions, attitude of the quarry, and even physical
differences among hunters. One of the most important preshooting
hunter exercises is to determine which eye is the stronger, the master eye.
A quick test is to close one eye. Most leave the master eye open. A more
complicated test is to cut a hole in a piece of paper and hold down while
you look at an object in the distance. Bring the paper up and the eye that
can see the object in the hole with the other eye closed is the dominant
eye. If you try to see the object in the hole with the closed eye, you are
probably a nonresident. Whether left or right, it's important to know
which eye is the one to aim with. For example, Buck shoots left-handed
and wipes powder residue from his master eye with his right hand (something he wouldn't have to do if he'd pony up for a new autoloader that
expels left). This cross-dominance is not the same as the cross-dressing
practiced by ducks' rights activists. If you are schooled in the East or are
any sort of mystic, you may have developed a third eye, which is difficult
to outfit with contemporary firearms.

Determining how much distance or "lead" to allow for your pellets
to reach the bird takes practice. A Blue-winged Devil will cruise by your
blind at 100 miles per hour, or 1,466 feet per second. If your pellets blow
out your barrel at 1,000 feet per second, it'll take one-tenth of a second
for you to realize that the top gun is already in the next county. Have a
nice day!

Determining the effective range is even more difficult for many
hunters. The experienced hand knows the right distance at which
enough shell shot will reach the quarry at sufficient speed to knock their
stuffing out so you can put your stuffing in. Beginners are encouraged to
learn range by taking the old blunderbuss out and blowing holes in paper

at different measured distances with different shot shells. This patterning method is great if you normally shoot paper ducks during the season (not to mention the papier-mâché decoys you shot last season). All water-fowlers need a foolproof hunting tool that can be used in the field; as expected, Buck has spared no expense to offer the latest range technolo-gy, field-tested by the rangy staff of the Dead Duck Society. Copy this special range indica-tor on acetate and use with the club's best wishes.

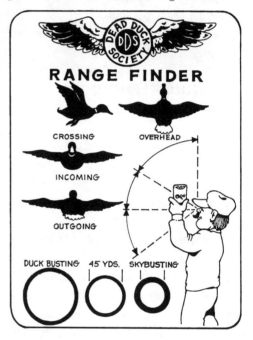

If you lose this invaluable aid, send whoever is on a large treasury note to Buck in care of the publisher for a replacement indicator and an eight-by-ten black-and-white glossy of Babe bathing in the lake. Until then, don't shoot ducks until you see their legs, honkers until you see the white patch, or your muzzle covers more than half of the bird!

HOW TO SHOOT FLYING GAME BIRDS

While Standing

There are three traditional ways to pop a cap at a duck or goose, with variations on each.

Swing-Through or British method

Shooters face and lock eyes on the flushed bird, position the feet with ten toes nine inches apart, or for careless shooters nine toes ten inches apart (some posture purists say the right foot of right-handed shooters should be off at 45 degrees), heels four inches apart, weight evenly balanced. Veddy good, old chap. While the muzzle is following the trajectory of the target, the gun is being mounted; as the muzzle passes through the bird, the trig-ger is pulled. Using the method favored by Churchill, never in the corn-field of conflict are so many ducks shot by so few hunters.

Sustained or "Pointing-Out" Method

The shooter establishes a lead, moves the muzzle at the same speed ahead of the bird, and fires when it feels right or before he or she corkscrews into the ground or bumps the barrel against the guide's head.

Snap Shooting

Used when a bird surprises a hunter nodding off in a heavy, warm waterfowl suit. With no time to spare, the shooter must react quickly and pick a spot in front of the bird where the pellets can meet with malice aforethought.

Premature Shooting

Not actually a method. The causes for premature shooting can be both mental and physical. See the club physician.

A radically different fourth method, as taught at Buck's Duck Hunting Lodge, is Buck's Original Nonconfrontational Shoot. Ducks do not like to be looked at and flare at the sight of a face, especially your face. Students of Buck's method turn their back toward the flight and fire over their shoulder, using a mirror and reverse lead. Reminder: Objects in the mirror are closer than they appear and smaller than they reappear in camp stories.

While Falling Down

If a shot is squeezed off as you step into a muskrat run, keep the barrel on the birds. Don't worry about leading the bird at this point. Your odds of hitting something are as good as in any of the above positions. What is most important is how you look. Fall forward with the muzzle pointed downrange and ahead of you. If you are falling backwards during a high overhead, land on your distended butt and assume the sitting position. There is no graceful way to fall on your back, so don't do it.

While Sitting Down

The sitting position is one of the hardest. If you are in a blind and a bird is about to bonk a decoy, some shooters say take your first shot sitting down. Once the ringing in your retriever's ears stops, your day of retrieving will have just begun.

While Lying Down

The prone position is used when the ground is too hard or time too short to dig a pit blind and the choices are either on your back or on your belly.

If you are on your back, you will have an unrestricted view of the sky directly above. One difficulty is that it's tough to shoot with the magnum recoil slamming your shoulder back into the dirt. The ground can be cold and wet and full of bugs, snakes, and cooties. You might lie down on the last endangered purple prairie titmouse, which is a felony punishable by reading game regulations without your magnifying glasses. Buck solves these problems by shooting from a reconditioned hospital bed powered by a twelve-volt battery and covered with a camouflage comforter.

If you are on your stomach and ready to fire away, either you are on a cliff shooting down at flying ducks or doing the four-point crawl on a pothole full of fat mallards. If the former, all Buck's good advice should be turned upside down. If the latter, a good sport allows birds to get off the water but not so high that the potholes can't become a potful of ducks.

WHICH BIRDS TO SHOOT

Rule 1. Shoot only the birds you can positively identify.

The first birds seen in the early-morning light will be quacking unidentified flying objects. To the inexperienced hunter, all birds will be seen as UFOs. Don't shoot them. UFOs were first recorded by the early Egyptian and Roman duck hunters but it wasn't until 1947 that the first UFO was reported on the Pacific Flyway. Actually it was a whole flock of them, flying near Mount Rainier. They are still seen from time to time, near the Hanford atomic waste dump.

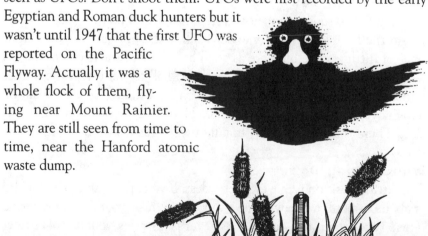

Rule 2. Shoot only the birds you can positively identify and positively hit.

BY DAWN'S EARLY FLIGHT

The earliest morning flights over the blinds on Big Babe Lake are by the Avian Air Force demonstration team, the Blue-winged Devils. Buck and Dorothy welcome the first flight of these flying aces and, from previous experience, do not even take a bead on the top guns under full power. The hotshots buzzing the stand are seen in groups of six: two solo birds and four fliers forming a diamond.

The first appearance is usually a warm-up fly-by that appears without warning directly overhead from the rear or from either side of the blind. On Big Babe Lake, the wake-up flight is at first light while Buck is having a cup of coffee and Dorothy is going through a jelly roll.

Delta Marsh Roll

The Delta Marsh Roll starts with the full formation coming from behind the blind, banking hard left, crossing the front of the command blind (CB), and exiting the flight line on a 45-degree rollout.

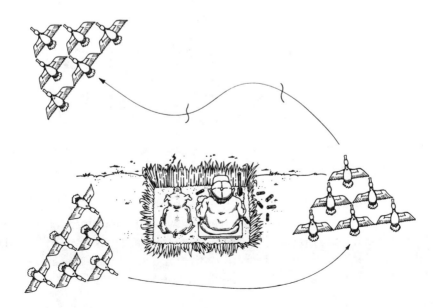

If the little Blue-winged Devils think you deserve a particularly good opener, they may start the show with the sun on their backs and in your face with the jelly roll break.

The Jelly Roll Break

The diamond reenters the flight line from the left, breaking left at 90 degrees into the sun for a 180-degree power turn to face the blind for a dramatic peel-off both left and right of the CB. At this point, the occupants of the command blind stop drinking coffee and eating jelly rolls (or rather one occupant has stopped drinking coffee) to concentrate on enjoying the performance.

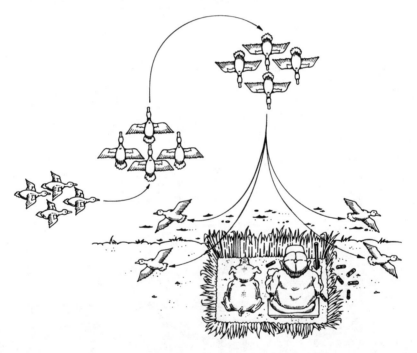

Now that they have your undivided attention, the aces bedevil you with air maneuvers that defy shot strings.

Opposing Four-Point and Tuck-Over Roll

To demonstrate individual flying prowess, the four birds of the diamond break into two pairs, the first to do a standard tuck-over roll upside down in section, then fly in front of the CB where they execute a 180-degree roll to the left and exit the flight line behind Buck and Dorothy.

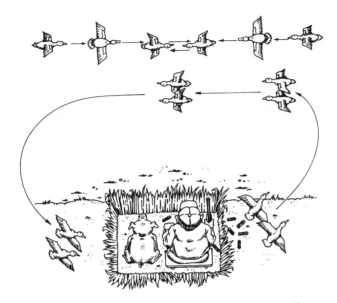

The second pair execute an opposing four-point roll to cross inverted for the waterfowlers.

For the last show of the morning, the Blue-winged Devils arrive out of the sun at three in-bound altitudes: numbers one and four at ten feet;

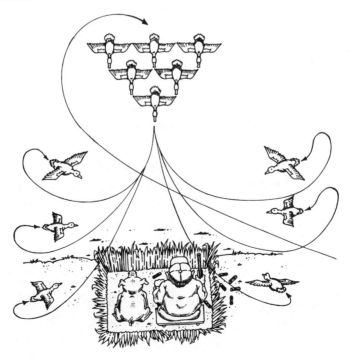

numbers two and five at twenty feet; and numbers three and six at thirty feet, with all birds exiting at fifty feet, just out of shot shell range, screaming at mach speed for altitude in the trademark exit maneuver, the famous Delta Marsh Vertical Break.

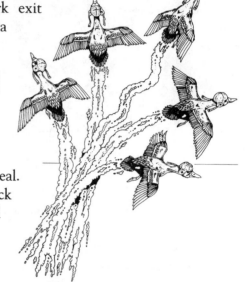

BUCK'S MEDICAL ALERT: The early-morning flight commonly causes whiplash, a severe injury that can take up to nine months (or next opening day, whichever is later) to heal. The strain includes both the neck muscles and ligaments, and necessitates a cervical collar and extended hours in the reclining position.

WHICH BIRDS TO SHOOT (CONTINUED)

Rule 3. Shoot drakes only.

Black duck hens, like many other puddler hens, fly point! A single mallard flying about Big Babe Lake is most likely a hen.

Rule 4. Shoot only the birds you want to eat (or mount).

The age of the bird is the important factor.

HOW OLD A DUCK SHOULD YOU SHOOT?

Game officials distinguish only between juvenile and adult game birds. They assume you wouldn't shoot ducklings unless there were enough to make a meal and you wouldn't be caught. It's difficult to age a bird in flight. Even if she could, a hen on the ground would never tell you the truth. Without bagging a banded bird and subtracting the date on the band from the current year, Buck relies on a few general behavioral and physical indicators for the three age categories: the juvenile bird, the adult bird, and the senior bird.

The Juvenile Bird

Thought to be a bird in its first year.

Behavioral characteristics: They trust you. They believe your calls and like your decoys. They may even like you. Too bad. They taste real good.

Physical characteristics: The tail feathers are notched on a youngster. Sometimes a juvenile will have molted late in the fall and look like an adult but if there is just one notched feather, the duck is still underage. If the birds are flying real close, eye color can be a determining factor. Young scaup females have brown eyes and hens three years or older (and all drakes) have yellow eyes. Often there is time in the blind for a personal inspection that shows juveniles of both sexes have what's called a bursa, which opens into the top wall of the cloaca and is lost in the first year. Buck would rather just have another cup of coffee.

The Adult Bird

Thought to be a bird that has paired and started a family.

Behavioral characteristics: They don't trust you. They don't believe your calls or like your decoys. They may not even like you. Too bad. They still taste good. Ducks in the wild do not time to have a midlife crisis. If a domesticated duck or goose has a midlife crisis, fly fishing doesn't help him complete the passage as much as the black dog waiting for him in the forest, a black Labrador retriever named Bart.

Physical characteristics: The tail feathers are rounded. The leg colors are brighter. The feathers are more colorful. The female has a conspicuous open oviduct between the opening for the large intestine and the left edge of the cloaca. The male has a, well, er, you know, a unit, a conspicuous unit that makes for a better mount, either on or off the mantel.

The Senior Bird

Thought to be a bird with an empty nest. Birds last longer in captivity. The oldest Canada goose lasted thirty-three years at home and only twenty-three years in the wild; a mallard will last twenty-three years in captivity and sixteen years in the wild. Which explains the rush to domestication.

Behavioral characteristics: They don't remember you. They didn't hear your calls or see your decoys. They certainly are tough to eat. Too bad. They still taste good. Parboiled.

Physical characteristics: All senses fade with age. Some birds go blind. The constant barrage of shotguns on fall migrations affects all surviving birds, which, like artillery veterans, have broken eardrums. Tail feathers are worn, broken, and missing. The skin sags and, in the puddle ducks, the foot arches fall. Drakes that survive the long migrations spend too much time attending species reunions of diminishing numbers; hens suffer from bladder infections caused by a lifetime of sitting in brackish water. Buck is sure all would prefer a nice hot bath (or parboil) if asked.

WHICH BIRDS TO SHOOT (CONTINUED)

Rule 5. Shoot the farthest bird first and work your way in.
Serious shooters start with larger, heavier loads and work their way in with lighter shot.

Rule 6. Shoot local ducks first.
The lazy buggers deserve it but don't shoot all of them! Early migrants tend to be unsuspecting and will land just to ask directions from the local yokels.

TYPICAL SHOOTING PATTERNS

Incoming
Some birds seem to invite themselves to the receiving end of a firing squad by flying straight at the shooter. They will be easy to identify. The common mistake is to shoot over the bird. Don't.

Crossing
Many birds come in from the side and decoying birds with lowered landing gear can easily be added to your game bag.

High Overhead
Lock in on the vapor trail and keep firing till you hit the bird or tip over.

Outgoing

A typical shot by many guests
of Buck's Duck Hunting Lodge
and the perspective of Babe's
waterfowl identification system. The
water near the nonresident blinds is
covered by tail feathers by day's end. A
common mistake is to shoot under the
bird. Don't! If shooting an over-under,
have the upper barrel pointing over and
the lower barrel under the bird.

MULTIPLE SHOOTING

How To Shoot Doubles

Buck shot a double of scaup as
they crossed midair not long ago and they
were as surprised as Dorothy was. But Dorothy politely harrumphed and
continued to go about her business, whatever her business was at the
moment.

How To Shoot Triples

This is tough with a single- or double-barreled gun, but if accom-
plished, guarantees membership in the Dead Duck Society.

How To Shoot Flocks

When describing a particular hunt to an absent buddy, more than
several birds is a flock even though the correct terminology is a plump of
waterfowl, a badelyng of ducks, a sord of mallards, a proud of pintails, and
a herd of swans. (Editor's note: "Hey, how did this get in here? You can't
shoot a herd of swans, especially out of season. Please disregard. Buck
must have been kidding.")

Ducks fly in flocks for selfish reasons, specifically to reduce the individual exposure to the predation of man during the open season. The
prevailing thought was that by changing flight positions often and pre-
senting a confusing sight picture, not only nonresident shooters but larger
sky raptors would pass on an unsure thing, much like a school of small fish.
Wrong! Flocks are shot by all four systems described above.

BUCK'S SPECIAL SHOOTING TIP: A common trait of all upright members of the Dead Duck Society is the ability to shoot oysters both in and out of season, with the same panache they use on shooting ducks. Sal Glynn, master oyster shooter and literary bluetick, maintains the life book of each member, with fresh lead in his ever-ready pencil. It's thought that this particular diet of ducks and oysters enhances the deserved pair-forming (though not pair-maintaining) reputation of the club membership.

What To Do If You Missed Your First Shot

Place your head between your legs. Touch your rear end with your fore end (practice makes this easier, sorta) because your next shots may require you to forcibly remove your head from your ventral area. If you don't learn how to do this yourself, others in the blind will assist you.

HOW TO KNOW IF YOU HIT A BIRD

If the bird's flight pattern is altered in any way, take immediate credit. The only danger to you and your duck-pig is if the trajectory of descent of a particularly large bird puts you at risk. Yell "Mark" and have Mark keep *his* head up to see where it lands!

HOW TO SHOOT SWIMMING ALMOST-ALIVE BIRDS

If the quarry drops in a near-death experience (NDE), you have an obligation to retrieve the emotional cripple. On water, you risk not only losing a bird that dives to safety and dies but also the health of your retriever swimming about in subzero waters. On land, you risk losing all your gear from overzealous officials hiding in the bushes with military scopes watching hunters not sacrificing their dogs on impossible retrieves. Diving ducks may not come up for a long time, some up to a minute, time enough for the game warden to use gray judgment about you not being sufficiently concerned about a wounded bird. Some birds will lay flat in the water; others, like redheads and bluebills, dive. Pintails will dive to the bottom and hold on. Smart shooters hit the wounded bird as it drops, as it hits the water, and when it first rights itself. Aim at its head with a wide pattern shot and keep shooting until it turns over.

HOW TO RETRIEVE A BIRD
A bird in the bush is worth two in the hand. At least that is how some officials interpret the Failure-to-Retrieve regulations.

How Buck Retrieves Ducks
He asks Dorothy if she's busy. If she is, he'll have someone send out a canine. If she's not busy, he'll still have someone send out a canine. Like Buck, Dorothy is a paragon of politeness and always lets the less fortunate have first shot.

How To Retrieve Geese
Don't even ask Dorothy! Retrieving a wounded goose on the water calls for the largest, strongest canine thug you can find. A dog must circle and attack the goose from below, pulling it underwater and drowning it. Retrieving a wounded goose on land is reserved for junior waterfowlers. It teaches the young why geese should be hunted and hunted and hunted.

HOW TO DISPATCH A BIRD
The most difficult part of the hunt is when you have to put down a bird up close. Remember two things: Any duck that flies within range of Big Babe Lake during open hunting season has suicidal tendencies to begin with, and any goose that's wounded wants to take you with it.

Humane Dispatch (Ducks)

- Bite back of neck and spine just below skull.

- Use a commercial "dispatcher" to part vertebrae of spine and separate windpipe.

- Bonk with a fisherman's priest.

Humane Dispatch (Goose)

• Grab it by neck and swing hard until something cracks.

The sportsman's ethic is important: If your brother-in-law was the shoot-er, don't let the bird see who knocked 'em down. That's plain inhumane.

CHAPTER 14

WHAT TO DO WHEN NO DUCKS ARE FLYING

HOW TO CALL DUCKS

You may have the perfect blind, the perfect decoys, and be hunting in perfect weather, but the ducks may not know you want to see them. The best way to announce your eagerness is to call them with a duck call.

Buck hunts all sorts of ducks, but the duck hen he hunts most goes "quack." Duck call manufacturers are proud to make calls that imitate a hen mallard, yet Walt Disney removed Daisy Duck's quacker by her sixth celluloid appearance as her anthropomorphized voice wasn't feminine enough. Walt's denial of Daisy's need to speak in her native tongue tells you a lot about the Kingdom.

Duck calls are typically of a resonate cavity design, with either a single or a double reed. They are made of plastic, rubber, or wood. They have been made from cane and beer tap handles. New calls can cost as much as several hundred dollars. Buck's last purchase was a clear plastic double-reed call. No sense putting a $200.00 call on a $19.95 mouth.

All call manufacturers advise beginners to practice before the season starts and some sell instructional tapes. If you want to sound like the home boys on the tapes, use the tapes. If you want to sound like game birds, practice with live game birds. And practice, practice, practice. Where should you practice? Anywhere they let you sing! In the shower, maybe. In the car, yes, alone with the windows rolled up and the sun roof closed but most certainly before the season begins!

How Long Should You Practice?

Look at it this way. It takes ducks less than three months to learn how to quack. When you compare the size of their brain and that of the average waterfowler, it's easy to see how long you should practice. Ten years max! If you consciously follow a master's informal instruction, you can shave nine years.

Specialists at Buck's Avian Research and Advanced Plucking Center have identified three primary calls made by ducks: the contact call, the warning call, and the call of attraction. Duck call manufacturers realize that beginners master the second call first and have focused on establishing a longer traditional sequence of calls used to contact and attract ducks in flight. Callers are not to move on to the next call in sequence until the home boys on the instructional record tell them, or unless birds respond by turning their heads, banking into a turn for a closer look, and/or returning the call, or their long-suffering hunting partner slaps the back of their head.

The Politically Correct Duck Calls (in traditional sequence)

The Hail or Highball Call

Used to attract birds threatening to land in someone else's decoys and any others in the fog thinking about it. The hail call starts off with a mouthful of loud quacks tapering off with softer, shorter quacks. Use the hail call until you see the birds dropping into the skybuster's decoys and then, and only then, for the sake of waterfowl conservation, have your American water spaniel stand up and practice its yodeling skills.

The Get-Down Call

Used to alert your partners to the flight arrival. This mouth call starts off with a soft "mark" followed by "birds at ten o'clock." All shiny faces still pointed skyward receive a slap to the back of each offending head.

The Come-On, Come-In, or Coax Call

Used to reinforce a good duck decision to land in your decoys. The cadence is about the same as the hail call but not as long or loud. At this point, the birds are usually committed to visit you regardless of how many waterfowl conservation shots are fired from the ol' skybuster's blind.

The Feeding Call

Used when the flock is close by. The premise of this call can only be followed until ducks are taught *not* to talk while they eat. One favorite call maker has a squealer call that ends with a high-pitched trailer sounding like a duck with a neck full of rice. In the more wild rice marshes of Big Babe Lake, Buck will use that squealer call, followed by his own patented choking-on-food call, and finishing with his custom throwing-up call.

The Comeback Call

Used when you see the ducks are not interested in your floating imitations or other offerings. This call of indignation starts as a come-on call and increases in volume and speed to an urgent highball call as they wing toward less shot-up decoys elsewhere.

The Lonesome Hen Call

Used when you are trying to attract a drake on the prowl or other hens on the water. Some callers use three quacks, the first slow and high-pitched, followed by two descending in pitch. Others suggest four to five single quacks, spaced a second or so apart. The difference is whether the lonesome hen is mated or not and how old she is. A young unmated hen sounds excited calling an attractive drake.

BUCK'S SPECIAL CALLING TIP: Use The Bawdy Duck® decoy with this call! An older unmated hen will be much more anxious, especially at closing time. An older mated hen just sounds crabby and that call is difficult to imitate.

The above sequence of calls is most often used to attract the greenhead puddle duck. The quack can also be used to attract less popular birds; manufacturers also sell calls that imitate many of the diver ducks. You can imitate some diving ducks by fluttering your tongue against the roof of your mouth through a mallard call. For that matter, you can flutter "brrrrrt" without the call and get the same results. What is difficult is quacking convincingly without a call. Buck tried this not long ago on a pair of decoying mallards and they broke into loose hysterics, which made it easier to shoot the drake. Life is good for the pure of heart.

A number of good-eating birds do not quack at all. Pintail, teal, widgeon, and wood duck drakes talk by whistling. The drake pintail has a soft, single-note whistle. All three teal have a whistle or peep of their own. The drake widgeon has a loud, nasal, three-note whistle, and the wood duck drake a soft whistle. For all of the above, all you need is an inexpensive whistle.

Many of the smaller diving hens don't have much to say at all (or their hubby can say it better) so if you are hunting hens, which you shouldn't, either just keep quiet or take the reed out of a call, blow through the open tube, and mouth the traditional calls. Old marsh rats like Buck don't even need a call. All the proper notes (or non-notes) can be reached by taking a deep breath and exhaling through pursed lips.

How Ducks Really Communicate

According to the latest studies in duck linguistics by the avian dunk tank and activist center, the Bordeaux Society (named after the house jug beverage and the subsequent headaches caused by too much tannin), duck-speak is not as simple as call makers make it out to be.

To understand modern quacking, a caller must first understand the differences in gender-based conversation. It's commonly held that drakes are more interested in giving out information or opinions, where hens are more comfortable in supporting others. As ducklings, hens learn to listen. Drakes using quacking as a means of gaining respect; hens use communication as a means of building and reinforcing community and relationships.

In the field and listening to Buck's records, Dorothy has noticed that when drakes talk to each other, the listeners try to one-up with more opinions like "the eel grass is better three miles away." This one-up drakeship is a reflection of a different social structure. Drakes like competitiveness and their rituals of assertiveness fulfill much of their need for intimacy.

When hens talk to each other, their quacks often overlap each other, indicating that either nobody is listening or everyone is so close they are finishing each other's conversation. Whatever the case, it's good to have a drake call handy to interrupt this incessant chatter.

What's most important in today's calling is knowing the different needs in duck communication and how to call within those specific requirements.

Situation: During migration, drakes rarely stop or call down for directions. By asking for specific travel information, drakes, especially the young bucks, feel they are admitting to a specific deficiency. Hens, however, enjoy the opportunity to chat with the local ducks about most anything.

Lesson: If you are calling migrating ducks, remember that drakes concentrate on the destination and stop only to eat and go potty. Use your feeding call and, if available, use your grunt call.

Situation: At the beginning of the day, drakes just want to feed in peace and quiet and read the morning papyrus. Hens, however, interpret this silence as rejection and try to engage the drake in a frisky conversation about most anything, even duck sports.

Lesson: If you are hunting the early hours and greenheads are flying in pairs, don't use a noisy hen mallard call, as the flying drake will think you are just a replay of breakfast.

Situation: At the end of the day, drakes do not want to talk about their day so do not use a hen call in a questioning manner. From time to time, drakes, especially those having domestic problems, will stop in friendly watering holes on the way home to talk drake-only stuff.

Lesson: Use a raspy drake call in the evening unless you are able to make a hen mallard call sound sultry. Several extra-raspy drake calls work best.

Other Tips On Good Calling

If you are calling juvenile birds, talk like they do: out of turn, giddy, with cracking voices. If you are calling senior ducks, don't stop calling them. They may forget why they're flying toward you. If they forget to try to land, keep calling, as it may come to them. If they land, they may not remember why they've landed, so keep up the feeding call until they start gumming marsh grasses.

If you plan to call in competitions, you'll have to quack your way through state, regional, and foreign quack-offs in order to blast the Hail, Lonesome Hen, Feed, and Comeback Call from a stage blind at the World Championship Calling Championships in Stuttgart, Arkansas. On his last visit, Buck slightly modified the second call and directed his Lonesome Drake Call toward the Dallas Cowboy Cheerleaders jiggling in front of the staging.

What If None of the Above Works?

Your calling might just be awful. Watch your partner's face when you start blowing. If he gives you an incredulous look, you may be doing either real good or real bad. If his expression turns to horror, it's bad. If he unloads his gun and sits down to have a cup of coffee and eat his sandwich, your calling is real bad. If the guide yanks the call out of your mouth, it's really, really bad.

Your call may just be out of order. All the advice on keeping it warm and dry went unheeded, didn't it? Take your call apart and blow directly at the reed assembly, using dental floss to remove any obstructions between reed and sounding board. If that repair doesn't do it, remove the reed holder and clean all the components before reassembling. Now the call may be out of tune. Duck call manufacturers seldom recommend tuning your own call for the same reason car manufacturers recommend you have warranty work done by fifty-dollar-an-hour mechanics.

BUCK'S DUCK CALLING TIP: Take out the old reed and push the new in as far back as you can. If the call is too low, clip the leading edge until you hit the right pitch. You've cut off too much if the final pitch is too high. Start over. If you don't have another reed, go home. It's getting too dark to shoot anyway.

ANOTHER THING TO DO IF NO DUCKS ARE FLYING
The birds might be hiding up- or downriver; put your bog hog and gear back in the canoe and hunt the moving water. Float up behind ducks by staying close to shore, quietly paddling and drifting along the near bank to the inside of a bend where ducks sit smugly in the quieter water. Sneak the river like you are hunting turtles, with the element of surprise in your hands.

Fat game birds might be hiding in isolated small waters off-river. Park the canoe and sneak up on the ponds and pools. Remember, for every duck you hear or see, there are more under the bank and in the brush. Buck and his little squirrel hunting buddy, Matt, sneaked up on a small pond full of willows one recent Minnesota opener and heard only one bird in the thicket. When we spooked that single loudmouth, another twenty quieter souls flew out the back door.

MORE THINGS TO DO WHEN NO DUCKS ARE FLYING

- Make fun of other people's camo.
- Pick up used brass.
- Take a leak.
- Fluff up blind materials.
- Pet dog.
- Tell lies.
- Rearrange decoys.
- Have a cup of coffee.
- Make more fun of other people's camo.
- Replace duck call reed.
- Go big job.
- Listen to guide's lies.
- Tell more lies than guide.
- Blow nose.
- Eat sandwich.
- Make snow angels.
- Shoot decoys.
- Make even more fun of other people's camo.
- Take a leak even if you don't have to.
- Tell more lies than anyone.
- Walk to rebuild circulation in legs.
- Blow dog's nose.
- Determine how cold it is.

How To Determine How Cold It Is

Air Temperature

If you are from northern Minnesota, "freezing" is 32 degrees below *centigrade!* Quit being such a baby. Embrace the cold. Dress for it. To Buck, thirty-ounce malone cloth is summer weight yard goods and, like many other northern Minnesotans, he spends a good portion of a year inside some sort of suit anyway.

Air Temperature + Wind = Windchill

If you are from northern Minnesota, windchill is just a temporary discomfort caused by facing the wrong direction. Turn around! Buck has a couple of freeze spots on his face from an early disregard but that hasn't diminished his taste for fine bourbon.

WHEN SHOULD YOU CALL IT QUITS?

The first thought of a serious waterfowler should be, "If the ducks can take it, why can't you?" Since Buck hunts with a fellow Scandinavian masochist who describes weather that even ducks avoid as "it could be worse," he uses a combination of two measurements to decide when to fold the tent: the ability to shoot and the color of his hunting partner's face. If the first condition is met by being barely able to get up and pull the trigger with or without gloves, turn toward your hunting pal and take a reading on the colors inside the hood of his parka:

If the face is pink and lips red, the wind is picking up. That's good. Ducks should start moving.

If the face is lavender and the lips violet, the wind may be changing directions. You should too.

If the face is orchid and the lips purple, it might be time to move the hand warmers around a bit.

If the face is white and the lips gray and you are hunting out of coffin blinds, you may not have to move at all.

CHAPTER 15

WHAT TO DO IF THE
ONLY BIRDS FLYING ARE GEESE

Buck hunts honkers too, two kinds of honkers: nonresident and resident. Each presents specific hunting opportunities.

HUNTING NONRESIDENT GEESE

Migratory honkers start moving out of Canada when the weather drops below freezing. When the temperature drops to zero, big birds jam the official flyway border crossings, much to the chagrin of immigration officials deputized to keep count.

Hunting by Creeping

An old Minnesota tactic is to creep up on a flock of unsuspecting honkers in an open field. Geese have their own sentries and the best time to creep is during the ceremonial changing of the guard. In one state, "it's unlawful to approach geese by creeping, crawling, or stalking for the purpose of taking geese or thereafter causing geese to be taken." That doesn't mean it's also unlawful to creep up on the patio of Café Du Monde in New Orleans to eat fresh beignets, washed down with dark-roasted chicory-flavored coffee.

Hunting by Pass-Shooting Over Decoys

Buck prefers to hunt honkers in open fields using a combination of full-sized and flat silhouette decoys, arranged in family groups of five to seven geese, six to eight feet apart, most feeding, with several in the sentry position. If the birds prove hard to decoy, waving black flags and adding loose black fabric to decoys might do it. There are commercially made goose kites but Buck prefers to fly a kite shaped like an eagle seventy yards overhead, forcing leery birds within range.

White geese are also hunted in open fields but with a different type of decoy. Adult snow geese are getting so wary that they won't necessarily respond to the typical assortment of white rags, paper plates, and diapers. Just from the diapers themselves, juvenile snow geese are often your only target and even they are requiring larger spreads. The problem with the guides using all that cloth down in Texas and Louisiana is that housewives hanging out bed sheets are decoying the larger birds into the suburbs.

Specklebellies are attracted to speckled bottoms so thrifty shooters solicit day-care centers for discarded speckled diapers. Put these decoys downwind!

Brant are pass-shot over parallel strings of full-sized decoys. If you actually get a chance to drop one of these magnificent birds, you may need a diaper, too.

HUNTING NONMIGRATORY GEESE

Buck's favorite honker hunt is for urban feathered freeloaders. Developers have long been fond of planning greenbelts to decoy condo and townhouse buyers into landing in their planned habitats. Even before the "stewards of the land" fold their tents and move on to fill another wetland, honkers homestead around the artificial ponds or shoreline. Stuffed full of pastries provided by well-meaning residents, these geese no longer need to forage for natural foods. Unfortunately, once a sugar-coated roll hits a loosey-goosey intestinal tract, the big bird produces at least a pound a day of goose doo, which produces complaints from raised-on-Disney urbanites who thought geese "hold it." At least that's how it seems on the Discovery Channel. Courageous local officials solve the problem by dumping it in another jurisdiction. Park geese are trapped during the molt and released in an area where they offend either a few voters, a less powerful official, or both.

To hunt these transplants, all you have to do is put a park bench near the water, set out your special Sam Blake urban goose decoys, and lock and load.

BUCK'S SPECIAL GOOSE HUNTING TIP: If you can prove serious crop damage from geese feeding on your land, you may be eligible for a special Agricultural Damage Permit, the thought of which gives hard-core honker hunters goose bumps!

WHAT TO DO WHEN NO GEESE ARE FLYING
Buck hunts honkers with a distinctive call. It sounds a lot like "herrr-onk-onk." Goose call manufacturers make calls that sound a lot like "herrr-onk." The calls look like either a regular duck call or a long flute. If you put a long fluted call on your lanyard, you'll look just like a honker hunter in the mirror. To your spouse, you'll just look goofy.

Do you actually need a goose call to attract honkers? Some of the best goose callers use only their own resonate chamber. Many harvest moons ago, Buck had breakfast with an experienced mouth caller in a packed midtown Manhattan eatery. Over runny eggs, the old gent mixed his herrr-onk with the other calls for attention in the air. His call of the wild attracted all sorts of attention, including the short attention span of the security guard at the door. We weren't that hungry anyway.

Goose specialists have identified at least ten different goose communications that all sound a lot like "herrr-onk."

- A loud all-purpose herrr-onk.
- An intimate spouse herrr-onk.
- A comfort herrr-onk to mate.
- A sharp herrr-onk to delinquent goslings.
- A postcoital herrr-onk.
- A herrr-onk of pain.
- A herrr-onk for help for lost mate.
- A herrr-onk for help for lost goslings.
- A herrr-onk of warning from the lead goose to stay in formation.
- A herrr-onk from the goose itching to give Buck's deeks a closer look.

Buck's custom herrr-onker is a stripped-down seventeen-key, six-ring clarinet done up in marsh camouflage.

When the master guide assembles his one-of-a-kind three-piece woodwind and gets on down with his souped-up interpretation of the highball herrr-onk (one herrr-onk, dramatic pause, then a pair of melodious herrr-onks), the ear holes of herrr-onk aficionados open up all around the county.

Any honker within frequency range immediately heads for the jam session and, with the crowd clearly on the way, Buck slides into his "hi, how are you?" herrr-onk, a shorter, more excited herrr-onk version of the highball. When the big birds cup their wings and circle, looking for the good concert seats, Buck's hunting partners pull out their double cluck calls and imitate feeding with excited rapid-fire clucks of varied lengths, pitches, and tones while the master guide returns his clarinet to the handsomely designed hard case lined with goose down from the previous season.

Buck doesn't need a comeback call. Any goose call now would only serve to wake the dead.

BUCK'S SPECIAL GOOSE HUNTING TIP: Your herrr-onk call will work for all honker subspecies, which goes to show you how smart they are and why they should be brought to heel. It's not hard to learn how to herrr-onk. Buck took his squirrel hunting buddy, Matt, to the top of a knoll in the middle of an alfalfa field and on the third try, this six-year-old's herrr-onk pulled a reply somewhere out of a low cloud on a fall day in central Minnesota.

In Buck's wild kingdom, few animals espouse monogamy and fewer are truly monogamous.

Biologists originally theorized that Canada geese mated for life because they were from Canada, where news of the more modern lifestyles seldom reaches. Unfortunately, studies by famous duck psychologists have revealed an alarming increase in Nordic depression in the honker population and the conditions sparking the depression, such as identification problems among subspecies, the cost of American cigarettes, and the erosion of moral fiber in the uniformed ranks of Environment Canada, will not reverse easily. The result: Experienced herrr-onk hunters like Buck are reporting increased numbers of male honkers purposely flying in range of the weaker steel shot.

HEY, BABY... DIDN'T I SEE YOU AT THE KLAMATH LAKE REFUGE LAST FALL? WHAT'S YOUR WINGSPAN?

The surprise: Newly widowed females in their winter homes are showing no interest in looking for another mate, which is a reason to blow them all into outer space and to send ol' Buck a Jackson for setting the record straight!

BUCK'S EXTRA-SPECIAL GOOSE HUNTING TIP: It doesn't make any difference if you shoot a male or female goose. What is good for the goose is good for the gander! Just pull the trigger.

CHAPTER 16

THE WRONG BIRD

WHAT IF YOU SHOT AND KILLED THE WRONG BIRD?
It's most likely that the hunting partner who claims all kills shot it. The wronged bird rightfully belongs in his bag limit. Put it there immediately.

If you retrieve the bird and keep it, a warden will magically appear to question you. Remove your Smithsonian membership card from your wallet and advise the uniform of your unofficial assignment to gather exhibit specimens for underprivileged children in dangerous inner city schools. A recent receipt from Safari Land or Birdland may also work here.

If your lame excuses don't work their intended magic on the uniforms gathered around your blind, you can count on being charged with one or more of the following offenses:

1. Failure to have a current hunting license.

2. Failure to have federal and state duck stamps affixed to the license.

3. Failure to sign the federal and state duck stamps with your real name.

4. Baiting
   Hunters cannot know that baiting has occurred in the area and cannot shoot over thrown rice in front of the chapel, even if a fellow waterfowler is taking the plunge.

5. Field Possession
   No hunter can have more than his limit in the field even while sorting out the best birds to take home.

6. Party Hunting

Hunters must not shoot at another person's birds, especially if they can't hit them. This applies to the skybusters
downwind and all nonresidents.

7. Tagging

All birds must be tagged with name of hunter, address of
hunter, species, date of kill, and a signed promise not to
overcook the bird.

8. Wanton Waste

Waste not, want not. Hunters must make a reasonable
effort to recover downed birds. The same day is a good start.

9. Rallying Waterfowl

It's illegal to frighten birds into the air with the outside of
your duck boat. What's inside your duck boat will be enough.

10. Chasing Wounded Waterfowl with Motorboats

Birds without disabilities can't swim faster than two to
three miles per hour on the water. With your duck boat
under power, there is a remote possibility that you are
engaged in what's discussed in number nine above. If you
are under power and trying to retrieve a bird, your gun
must be empty and in its case and you must be fully zipped.
In northernmost Minnesota, once you ram the bird with
your boat, the motor must be stopped and all forward
motion ceased before you conduct the memorial service.

TYPICAL PUNISHMENTS

Delinquent hunters are taken by a peace officer to the court in the county of violation where someone's brother-in-law sees your out-of-state
plates and gavels you guilty with the following penalties:

First violation: $700 and/or 90 days.

Second violation: $700 and 90 days.

If you have committed all ten violations, the verdict is $7,000 and/or 900
days in the pokey. Unless you have that much vacation time coming, just
pay the judge. For those who need a real vacation, take the time and ask
the judge to deny conjugal visits.

In some states, the punishment for both minor and major infractions is the requirement to buy the state waterfowl print, which is enough for real art lovers to choose imprisonment.

In Canada, nonresident hunters are given summaries of hunting regulations. For complete information on such things as general prohibitions, contact the enforcement coordinator of Environment Canada. The telephone number is included in the summary should your cellular phone be with you in the blind. With the cost of a nonresident license, it's assumed that you can call collect. If you can't interrupt their personal calls and do something wrong anyway, remember the bold print of their summaries:

SIGNIFICANTLY HIGHER FINES FOR HUNTING VIOLATIONS MAY BE IN EFFECT THIS YEAR

What could you do wrong? The most common mistake is to assume that Canadian bag limits are tied to the value of their currency. If an American dollar buys $1.30 in Canadian currency, do not assume your daily bag of six ducks and five geese jumps to seven-and-a-half ducks and sixteen geese. The second most common mistake is to try to tip the game wardens in Canadian money. In the more remote areas, officials require hard currency and/or American shotgun shells in payment to smuggle your birds out of the country in a diplomatic pouch. The third most common mistake is to act badly in their public places: Those errors in judgment are expected from a nonresident, especially one full of their ale.

In the key hunting areas, most sentencing occurs in drive-through double-wide trailers, inside of which tourists can buy firewater, maple sugar candy, and baby seal skins.

Fines for minor infractions are easy:

Promise not to do it again.

Five Canadian loonies or six American dimes (whichever is greater in value at the time of infraction).

Spouse in custody.

For major infractions, expect the worst:

Possession of your boat, shotgun, and vehicle.

Release of spouse in custody.

If you've violated Canadian game laws *and* offended the Queen, the court may require you to rub noses with a woman of First Nation at the next treaty negotiation. At that point, Buck recommends calling the local United States Embassy.

BUCK'S SPECIAL CANADIAN HUNTING TIP: | Canadian telephones take slugs!

WHAT IF YOU SHOT AND SERIOUSLY WOUNDED THE WRONG BIRD?

In some states, you not only pay the fine for the infraction, you must also pay restitution for each really wronged bird. For example, if you wrong a bald eagle in Minnesota thinking it was a baldpate, you will pay an additional $2,000 to the state (you can probably make some of that back by selling tail feathers to the local reservation chiefs). If you accidentally wrong a mama loon *and* the babies on her back, you will be chained to the center post of the Mall of America for an entire holiday season. If you are one mallard over the limit, you will cough up whoever is on a fifty-dollar bill. So it's important to know emergency life-saving procedures. Save your hide by saving theirs!

Mouth-To-Beak Resuscitation

For a Small Duck

Put your mouth over the whole beak and the top of the head and breathe in and out a dozen times as fast as a duck normally breathes. That should do it. If it doesn't, pull out your Smithsonian card and get back down on your knees.

For a Large Bird

Put your mouth over the slightly opened beak and your fingers over the nostrils as you breathe in and out. If the bird recovers, be prepared to protect your own beak.

For a Shell Shot Broken Wing or Leg

Your first obligation is to get that bird walking, flying, or floating away from your blind as soon as possible. Bind the appendage with Ace bandages, splints, and, as a last effort, a Styrofoam raft.

WHAT IF YOU SHOT AND KILLED BUCK'S HANDMADE WOODEN DECOYS

You won't need toothpicks for the wood duck he'll serve you.

WHAT IF YOU SHOT AND KILLED A LEGAL GAME BIRD?

Hooray! At last! Time to go home!

CHAPTER 17

TAKING DUCKS HOME

There are three reasons to take ducks home:

To eat.

To mount.

To be recognized by the Boom and Crockpot Club.

If you are taking birds home to eat, be aware of the ranking of desirability. Purists say that you can eat anything that has a digestive tract; then again, there is no purist recipe for eating old coots.

WHO GETS WHICH DUCKS?

If you and your hunting party each have a limit on the tailgate and it's time to split up the birds, who gets which ducks?

Announce your management of the distribution by stacking the birds in equal piles. Place the more aerated or drafty ones in the sky-buster's stack, commenting sotto voce that the shots may have been good ones but those magnum loads really chewed up the birds.

Determine who will want to take birds home. Some newlyweds may not want to return with any evidence of the hunt.

For those whom you know like to eat fish, tell them that by taking the sea and diving ducks, they can have their fish and eat their duck, too.

If the distribution doesn't come out exactly even, ask the guide or non–duck eaters for some (or, in the case of the guide, all) of theirs. Which species to put in your pile? With wide variations, depending on what each species is eating, the best-eating ducks found on Big Babe Lake are listed in order of availability:

1. Mallard

2. Wood duck

3. Green-winged teal

Flatheaded flatlanders argue that puddlers are better tasting than diver ducks. Nonsense. All ducks taste good, just different. In Buck's view, the better-eating diver ducks are pintails, widgeons, and redheads. The best-eating geese are young Pacific brant fresh out of Padilla Bay in northwest Washington. The effort to take a limit of brant is worth it.

Ducks Not To Put In Your Pile

Ducks that eat asparagus
Don't even clean them. The insides of a bird that eats this green vegetable smell like a toilet.

Ducks That Are Sick
Buck once opened an ailing duck that was part of a pile of puddlers and didn't notice the green stomach until he had already lifted the hatch cover.

Ducks That Wear Leg Bands
In his more impressionable years, Buck would wear yards of leg bands wrapped around his neck and have to be personally escorted around the metal detectors at major airports. Ducks that can be trapped by banders are not the truly wild birds of Big Babe Lake and are a symbol of an easy shoot.

Ducks To Put In Your Pile
Ducks That Sport Magnum Curled Undertail Covert Feathers
Possession of these feathers will allow you the opportunity to be considered for membership in the oldest conservation organization, served by the staff of the Vallhalla Lounge.

TRANSPORTING GAME BIRDS

Once the birds have been divvied up, hunters have a choice of cleaning them in the field or at home. Some hunters may have been offered explicit instructions on this matter before they pulled out of the driveway.

If you decide to field-dress your birds, regulations require that all migratory waterfowl retain a fully feathered wing and head while they are en route to your kitchen.

HEN   DRAKE

All the feathers should be saved in the order they were removed if you decide later to have a taxidermist mount these field-dressed birds. Supplicants for the Boom and Crockpot Club must retain the curled covert feathers of the drake mallard.

THE BOOM AND CROCKPOT CLUB

The large majority of guided shooters and press freeloaders hunting Big Babe Lake have a membership interest in this most prestigious (and pri-

vately held captive) waterfowl conservation organization. With roots in
a dimly lit, steamy, sweat lodge rite involving handsome Viking warriors
and sorta willing buxom native women, the Boom and Crockpot Club
was formed in the halcyon days of market hunting by a few waterfowlers
concerned that less desirable ducks were being discarded in the restau-
rant triage. Central to the club's conservation principles is the
philosophy of Fair Catch, which provides that all ducks and geese be
taken in hot pursuit, and that all that falls from the sky is caught and
cooked. Fair Catch guidelines state that cormorants, mergansers, and
shiedpokes be included in nonresident game bags.

The club is well known for its endowment of the Boom and
Crockpot Bar Stool in Advanced Plucking at the University of the Great
Loon Spirit, Nevis, Minnesota, and its sponsorship of the national measurement standards of the magnum drake mallard. The club is best known
for its high post-hunt glee and, to keep a semblance of order during happy
hour, an awards program was designed to recognize the trophy quality of
a Big Babe Lake hunt and promote Fair Catch.

Scoring of all entries is by Babe's system of measurement as practiced at the pouring stations of the Vallhalla Lounge. A shooter makes a
preliminary measurement in the blind and, if a blind majority concurs, a
trophy entrant can be brought into the Vallhalla Lounge for measurement. An official measurement cannot be made by Babe and her official
Lounge Measuring Staff until the shooter has bought the entire bar six or
a half-dozen (whichever is larger) rounds of premium-brand chasers. No
house labels, at full price Fridays, Saturdays, and all holidays. Happy-
hour prices on weekdays only. Multiple entries must be chased by a lethal
concoction from Saunder's South Forty East Substation: the Duck Pfart
(one shot Kahlua, one shot Bailey's Irish Creme, splash of Canadian
whiskey on top, and served over ice).

Only entries thus fairly chased are eligible for awards. Curled coverts
must be attached to the bird as it's easy enough to retrieve unattached
coverts near the nonresident blinds. Only trophies taken on Big Babe
Lake are eligible for entry. Undersized trophies of unknown origin will go
into the Lounge's kitchen crockpot. The Club reserves the right to reject
any entry and eject any applicant who fails to fully satisfy the high personal standards of the organization. This includes any nonresident bring-
ing in a mallard hen breast to be measured for the booby prize.

Officious Scoring System For Buck's Big Ducks

Records of North American Big Ducks as kept in the Valhalla Lounge, Buck's Duck Hunting Lodge on Big Babe Lake, northernmost Minnesota.

TYPICAL MAGNUM MALLARD CURLED COVERTS

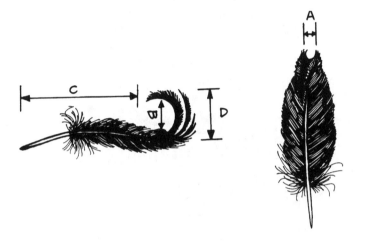

A. Inside Spread: minimum 5 mm
B. Greatest Spread: minimum 10 mm
C. Length of Main Beam: minimum 100 mm
D. Circumference of Short Curly Hairs: minimum 35mm

Final Score:
Minimum score 150 mm

Upon confirmation of score, the owner will be entered in the Big Score
Book kept under lock and key by the organization and accorded the good
will and heartfelt thanks of those members in good standing, er, rather,
still standing at the bar.

CHAPTER 18

EATING DUCKS AND GEESE

One of the best things about hunting ducks is that you may have a chance to eat one. Buck likes to eat duck at any time of the day: He likes his breakfast duck ground into chorizo with eggs and hash browns; at lunch, smoked and sliced on an open-faced sandwich; a little duck pâté before a midafternoon nap; and an evening of big marsh dining. Buck eats only wild duck and the wilder the better. He thinks the only way to stop the enthusiasm for the domestic dolts is to eat their young by oeuffing them in the morning. The occupants of the thick-shelled domestic duck egg fry up harder, but you'll be doing a good deed.

Once the duck hunters return from the blinds with their bounty, Babe and her staff in the kitchens of Buck's Duck Hunting Lodge offer several methods of handling the wild game.

General Preparations

Where To Clean

Clean birds outside, down by the river, out in the garage, or upwind of pesky neighbors. *Warning!* Do not clean your birds in your guest room! Buck once tried to clean a limit of birds in a motel in eastern Washington before the maid came into the bathroom. There is *no* way you can power flush wings and entrails that fast without feathers everywhere.

When To Clean

Immediately. If the hunger is there, Buck cleans, heats, and eats his birds right on the spot, outside the blind.

Hung Around For a While

Old World enthusiasts and aristocratic originals prefer to hang their fowl before preparing for the kitchen. There are two grade schools of thought (and too much gallows humor) on the hanging: From the neck until the guts fall out; from the feet until the eyes pop out.

 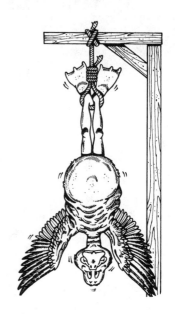

The hanging must be in cool surroundings: below 40 degrees in the shed or above 40 in the refrigerator for a week to ten days. The enthusiasts of the latter hanging want the entrails to fall into the breast cavity, adding even more flavor to the meat. The bird is and hung until the stomach skin starts to turn color.

How To Clean

There is peculiar language surrounding this step in the preparation of a duck dinner. Upland bird hunters dress their birds for cooking but then again, upland bird hunters dress themselves funny. At the Lodge, Buck undresses his birds for cooking, then undresses himself for goosing the young birds out in the hot tub.

At this point, it's best to be sure the duck is deceased. Place a mirror over the beak to see if the bird is still breathing. An old English superstition holds that if someone who is ill inhales duck breath, even dying duck breath, the complaint will disappear. Buck has smelled duck breath and verifies that all other problems pale in comparison. If the critter is still alive, don't shoot the bird in a busy kitchen. Just feed it some leftover holiday fruitcake or lutefisk. It won't take long.

Assuming the fowl has passed through the pearly gates and you have closed the eyelids, there are several outer garment options.

To Pluck

Plucking feathers is best left to the junior members of the hunting party but they at least have the option of either dry- or wax-plucking. It's easiest to dry-pluck warm birds. In northern Minnesota, thaw the late-season birds first. Starting with the breast, pull feathers in the direction they grow and then work around the body. If you have a bunch of birds, melt a block of paraffin or last year's Christmas candles in a double boiler and dip the bird in the hot wax. Once cool, the waxy feathers can be peeled off. Burn off any leftover fuzz with a torch. If you can't wait for a snack, use the torch a little longer.

To Skin

To skin a bird, just cut around the neck and pull down on the feathered jumpsuit.

Some hunters just reach through the skin and remove the breasts only, while others skin the entire bird. If you decide to breast a bird, note that hens who have had children lose the perky breasts of their youth and only trophy birds that nest in California's Silicone Valley maintain a shapely figure. To breast out a bird, cut an opening in the skin with a thin sharp knife and open like a jacket. Cut along both sides of the breastbone, turning out at the rib cage. On sea ducks, first cut under the wings where the skin is looser.

BUCK'S HEALTH ALERT: Some waters have food chains choked with PCBs. You shouldn't eat any mallards, black ducks, scaup, or ruddy ducks from the Milwaukee harbor unless you've had too much beer made from the same waters. In any industrial area, remove and discard the skin and any visible fat and do not use the pan drippings unless you want gravy that glows in the dark.

Once the bird has been defeathered or skinned, it's time to reach deep inside the stomach and chest cavity to pull out all the insides. At first glance, the private parts are messy but not indecent like those of a certain New York radio personality. Save the heart and gizzards for stock. Amputate the head, wings, and feet. Carve out any shot-damaged tissue. Wrapped in the delicate skin that crisps to a golden brown, the bird is now ready for the oven. The age will determine the cooking method. Buck soaks questionable birds overnight in buttermilk. Hesitant young birds may need to soak a couple of hours in the Lodge hot tub to soften up.

Marinades are your first opportunity to add extra flavor to the cooking process. Whatever you do, remember that duck doesn't taste like the bean curd found on most meat market counters and most important, duck does *not* taste like chicken. Duck can be enhanced by soaking in a favorite salad dressing, red wine, or even bourbon. Even Buck himself has been enhanced by a fine sour mash.

SIMPLE RECIPES

Who cooks the birds? Family tradition normally determines that whoever is in the kitchen preparing regular meals does the cooking, but the uncertainties involved in cooking game meat may alter the workforce. If you don't do a good job cleaning the birds, you will get full cooking privileges, unless of course you walk into the Tiffin Hill test kitchen with a can of Campbell's cream of mushroom soup. Respect your duck!

You don't need a large lodge kitchen like Buck's, even though his kitchen has received many citations from the local health authorities. All the meals at Buck's Duck Hunting Lodge are prepared as the help scratches and require only common utensils.

Buck's ducks are ready to eat with only a fast roast in a very hot oven. The bird doesn't have to be stuffed, seasoned, or covered with hickory-smoked bacon to taste good. Just cooked real hot, real fast. A hot cooking seals in the juices. A recent cleaning of Buck's game locker revealed a week's worth of puddle ducks just this side of freezer burn and for each night, one bird was quick-roasted as described. A ducks-only diet is what it's quacked up to be! There are many cookbooks

available on how to prepare waterfowl and
the best selections are in stores that sell
both new and used books. One of the sim-
plest and very best cookbooks is James
Beard's *Fowl and Game Bird Cookery*, if for no
other reason than his recipe for "Wild Duck in
the Mud." If cooking wild duck makes you
(and your guests) nervous, use this inexpensive paperback and drop this famous baker's
name as needed.

Buck recommends that you cook duck
like you shoot duck—by winging it! The great
but hard-to-find scope manufacturer, Waldo
Leopold, once said that it's in the kitchen that the ethics of the hunter
are in best evidence. "A particular virtue in wildlife ethics is that the
hunter has no galley gallery to applaud or disapprove of his conduct.
Whatever his acts, they are dictated by his conscience and a need not
to overcook duck."

Duck á L'Range

Duck meat is lean and flavorful and needs no assistance from culi-
nary enhancements.

Preheat oven to 400 degrees F. Stuff an undressed duck with one cup
chopped celery, one cup chopped onion, and one quartered apple or one
peeled and sectioned orange. Place duck in roasting pan and drape four
pieces salt pork or smoked bacon over breast. Bake or roast the bird for an
hour or until done, then serve. For those on different schedules, reduce
heat to 325 degrees F and bake for two hours or until done. The bird can
also be placed in a oven baking bag and cooked at 250 degrees F all afternoon or until you and the other birds in the hot tub start to shrivel up.

Prick bird to test for doneness. If juices are just a little pink, and
internal temperature is 150 degrees, the duck is medium rare and ready
to eat. If the bird's internal temperature is 180 degrees, it's well done and
too done for Buck.

Time will vary according to the size of the bird and how steady the
source of heat. While cooking, you may find it impossible to leave well
enough alone, so while your head is in the oven aspirate the fat off the

pan bottom with a bulb baster every twenty to thirty minutes and baste as needed.

BUCK'S SPECIAL COOKING TIP: Basting materials are the swing ingredients in the final taste of your bird. It's easiest to use the fat on the bottom of the pan. James Beard recommends adding a rich burgundy. Beard also suggests a mixture of honey and curry powder for domestic ducks, but those white eunuchs don't deserve the attention. Give it to your wild ducks. A Canadian Buckster may use maple syrup or rye whiskey. For a sweet glaze, slather on one cup of your favorite berry jam or orange marmalade. Judy Blake glazes with a mixture of ¼ cup honey, ¼ cup sugar, and a cup of orange juice. Buck glazes a duck skin pressed with fresh ground black pepper with ½ cup Paul Prudhomme's Hot Barbecue Sauce or jalapeño jelly.

BUCK'S EXTRA-SPECIAL COOKING TIP: The son of a baker and point man for many of Buck's sorties in the Big City blasts his bastes into his birds using custom loads with special seasonings rolled into the shot mix like a Parker House roll. Not FDA approved, but how much is these days?

FRENCHY'S CHICKEN-FRIED DUCK

Accompaniments for duck run from the traditional wild rice to steamed white rice with crisp and colorful fresh vegetables. Buck prefers to eat more wild duck than fill up on tame accompaniments. He starts with a duck salad made with warm roast duck strips, chopped walnuts, crumbled blue cheese, and mixed greens drenched with a warm and spicy vinaigrette dressing, then waits for the renegade "Frenchy" to grace the informal chef's table with another of his in-season masterpieces.

In a large skillet, heat two tablespoons olive oil and sauté one cup sliced mushrooms until brown. Set mushrooms aside. Roll two duck halves in a mixture of two tablespoons flour and salt and pepper and braise in skillet until rare. Set duck halves aside and add to skillet ¼ cup dry red wine, two tablespoons Johnny's All-Purpose Seasoning Sauce, and two tablespoons Worcestershire sauce. Slowly stir in one cup heavy cream and heat thoroughly. Add the mushrooms and duck halves and cook over low heat until duck is medium rare.

TOO TUFF TO STUFF

In a roasting pan, braise or brown any duck, any age, on all sides. Add red wine to the pan until the level is halfway up the bird. Cover and simmer until tender. Cool, slice, and serve with hot mustard, sesame seeds, salsa, horseradish, or blue cheese dressing. If you want to try something different, add the ingredients of a good gumbo to the duck as it is simmering. Buck gives high Marx to duck soup, too!

SMOKED DUCK

In the bottom of a roasting pan, split an undressed duck and place on a small wire mesh rack. Place a handful of trimmings from an apple tree branch on the bottom of the pan. On a hot burner, place the pan with the cover slightly askew for about twenty minutes and you'll have "smoked" your duck twice!

As evidenced by the author photo (see page 188), Buck's freezer is full of fat, corn-fed mallards. Occasionally, a diver or sea duck, whose principal diet is either fish or shellfish, will end up in his game bag. Some dabblers think that a preference for seafood taints the meat and that divers should be specially treated. Some even suggest soaking the bird in salt water overnight, which seems punitive since those ducks have been soaking in salt water all their lives. Buck believes that sea ducks eat seafood just to be unpalatable to mallard huggers; he foils them by cooking divers or sea ducks according to the taste of their flesh.

For oyster-eaters like pintails and widgeons, Buck respectfully roasts them stuffed with their preferred meal chopped in a tasty stuffing.

For fish-eaters, Buck prepares the ducks like fish: baked, breaded, broiled, pan-fried, poached, sautéed, or steamed; in a dark gumbo; as "can-cakes"; or in traditional gastronomical garb as a Merganser Meunière, a Scauplette en Brochette (scaup breasts cut to scallop shapes), or Scaupi (scaup breasts filleted like scampi).

BUCK'S BONUS DIVER RECIPE:

BUFFALO-HEAD WINGS

First shot at anchor on an offshore bar, these diver duck spare parts are post-game comfort food for a threatened resident population of bills along the upper Atlantic flyway. Dive for five!

Preheat oven to 375 degrees F. Cut two dozen buffalo-head wings into two pieces each, cut off tips, and salt and pepper to taste. In a heavy cast-iron pot, heat four cups olive oil and cook half of the duck wings until brown, remove and drain, then cook the other half and remove and drain. Place duck wings in a serving dish. In the pot, melt g cup butter and add four tablespoons Frank's Louisiana Hot Pepper Sauce and one teaspoon white vinegar, mix well, and heat thoroughly. Pour over wings. Serve wings with chilled celery sticks and dip in chilled blue cheese dressing. Send out for more postgame comfort beverages.

EATING GOOSE

Why Eat a Goose?

There is a long history of eating geese that lay any eggs, much less golden ones. In olden times, the breast was served to the royal family with the hind end reserved for the servants, a practice that contributed might-ily to palace revolutions. Goose dining traditions do not limit themselves to just the delicious exteriors. Foie gras or fat goose liver is haughty cuisine and the bird selected to donate that organ for gastronomic research is overfed until the liver reaches optimum size. Given the gentle nature of the bird, Buck recommends auger-feeding every domestic goose until the liver (or for that matter, anything else) pops alienlike from the abdomen. Goose tongue was once thought to be an aphrodisiac; then again, so were swan genitals, which gives new meaning to the term *swan song*. The giblets and other sweetmeats are common ingredients in gravies and pâtés. In Scandinavia, even goose blood is used as the base of a soup.

THE SINGLE MOST IMPORTANT REASON TO EAT A GOOSE IS THAT THEY WOULD EAT YOU IF THEY HAD THE CHANCE!

There was a rural sport in the early 1800s called gander pulling, which involved horsemen trying to jerk the greased head off a domestic gander tied to a tree. This game should qualify as an Olympic event for anyone who has had an aggressive domestic goose flare up on him!

Domestic geese are part of many hobby and working farms. Without predators, these geese get fat and territorial. Unless you are a resident, more specifically an occupant, there is no open hunting season on these big fat birds. One of the very few opportunities to harvest a domestic goose is with your four-wheeled shopping cart out on the public county road. Nonresident, or more specifically nonoccupant, road-hunting privileges are prohibited in the driveway to the farmhouse unless the occupants aren't home.

Waterfowlers have one sure way to get all the geese they can eat. By shooting them. With few exceptions, wild goose populations are healthy and growing. To most hunters, geese are just big ducks and are prepared and cooked the same way. The big difference in cleaning a goose is the presence of down, an insulation layer that is thick enough to allow these big birds to sleep on the tundra and fly at 10,000 feet without relying on today's synthetic materials.

Buck likes to eat goose as often as possible. The occasion of a goose as an entrée has always been formal and festive. In Charles Dickens's *A Christmas Carol*, Bob Cratchit thought the "tenderness, flavor, size, and cheapness" of his family's holiday goose "were the themes of universal admiration." The main character, Ebenezer Scrooge, tumbles through three stages of an opium hangover and tries to buy his way out of a time warp with a prize turkey, an early example of the persuasive strength of the United Turkey Growers Confederation. Another old tale is that he who eats goose on Michaelmas Day, September 29, will never lack money to pay his debts. St. Michael's day was the day to pay the quarterly rent and the exchange of a goose commemorated the day until rent control was introduced.

The size of a goose is more important to the shooter than the eater. In the kitchen, the age of the goose or gander is what guides the chef.

YOUNG GOOSE

To cook a young or juvenile bird, seal in the juices with high heat and then cook to desired wellness.

> *Preheat oven to 400 degrees F. Clean, stuff, and season one goose. Place goose in roasting pan and reduce heat to 325 degrees F. Bake or roast for an hour or until done, then serve. Baste with pan drippings every twenty to thirty minutes and/or as needed.*

OLD GOOSE

To cook an old bird, give up looking for any juices to seal in. Pound, soak, and marinate the muscles until they can be cooked.

The meat on old Mother Goose is normally so tough from flying around reciting turgid, meaningless verses to suffering little children that Jack Sprat is often the only one able to lick this platter clean. Special preparations are necessary to soften this old bird so little Tom Tucker can cut it without e'en a knife. Buck recommends a recipe from deep down in bayou country, where Eli says "Blueberry Hill" is still

number one on the jukebox and coonasses don't go where they can't sit on Igloo coolers full of longneck Budweisers, congregatin' around big pots of goose gumbo.

Remove old goose breasts, butterfly the meat, and pound with back of dinner knife. Soak breasts in salt water for thirty minutes, rinse, and dry. Transfer breasts to a bowl, cover with orange juice, and let marinate for two to three hours. Remove breasts from juice and drain. Preheat broiler. Sprinkle breasts with Lowrie's All-Purpose Seasoning, roll up like a jelly roll, and wrap with thickly sliced hickory bacon. Sprinkle on a little Worcestershire sauce and broil to medium rare. Enjoy the goose's just desserts!

HERRR-ONK IF YOU LOVE TO EAT GOOSE!

CHAPTER 19

AFTER THE HUNT, THE MEAL, AND THE SEASON

All good things must come to an end. With birds in the freezer, it's time to hang the hip boots, empty the jacket and pants pockets of loose shells, oil the gun for the cabinet, and wash the mud off the boat and decoys. Dorothy rests easy knowing Buck takes care of these important details and spends much of her time in front of the Lodge fireplace sorta thinking about great duck hunting. An end-of-

season armistice has been declared on Big Babe Lake and thoughts naturally turn to the celebrations of the holidays. The birds not in the freezer really appreciate a special day since, unfortunately, many of the traditional holidays are based on celebrations of a harvest, to wit:

The start of the season, or *Los Dias de Muertos*, is the scariest part of the duck's year.

On Halloween, the night of the dead, humans dress up in clothes that look like marsh grass and wise ducks fly under a full moon rather than at high noon.

The most important duck holiday, Veteran's Day, is celebrated at the end of the migration for the early migrants and later for any others. The reunions are distinguished by a brief memorial service and a lingering respect for the ground artillery emplacements around Big Babe Lake. The battlefields are revisited by the curious on the return migration.

Thanksgiving has not been celebrated by ducks since the first harvest festival when the Pilgrim governor "sent four men out fowling." As can be expected, the Pilgrims shot like typical nonresidents and Squanto had to requisition more venison for the table.

Christmas, however, is another story. In this, the jolliest time of the year, Buck sets down his spiked eggnog and returns to the cattail marsh to call his little duck-billed buddies home for the holidays. He is often joined by his alpha ducks, Biff and Eddie, and backed by the Big Babe Lake Brass and Bong Ensemble. Bucksters and other lodge guests

are invited to sing seasonal favorites along with Buck's Ducks on the
festooned log deck off the Valhalla Lounge.

WHY DOES
BUCK HUNT DUCKS?

To hunt ducks you must leave your comfortable, predictable surroundings for that less familiar place where ducks work their magic. Real ducks don't live in the city parks. Their spell is cast only where they—not you—call home, and once there, you will refresh your soul and rediscover a simple passion.

When you visit or return to a marsh, shore, field, or river, you may not seem to remember as much as you'd like, but once birds start cupping their wings all your senses will return in an undeniable, unforgettable rush. You will hear air moved by by invisible wings. You will smell both the warm and the cold. You will search the skies for ducks and see geese and swans and bald eagles and blue herons and brown pelicans. You will never feel more out of your world as you wait in suspense for honkers hovering just out of range on wings creaking like old leather, or as you are surprised by a pothole full of greenheads. You will never feel more in their world as an ermine sticks its nose out of snow bank while you're floating a river for late season goldeneyes, or as a beaver slaps its tail in a territorial misunderstanding. On those honest, healthy singleminded days in the field, you will feel the sunrise on your forehead and the wind shift on your cheek and the day will be interrupted by the sunset.

It's in this world of magic that Buck hunts and where a hunting pig is not out of place.

"Buck" Peterson and Dorothy his hunting pig stand in front of Buck's duck shack on the Great Cattail Marsh of Big Babe Lake. The Minnesota Hysterical Society has announced plans to preserve the improperly seasoned building for future degenerations. No one has announced plans regarding the improperly seasoned occupant, citing too much preservative already added.

PRINTER'S NOTE

This limited printing of *The Compleat Waterfow(u)ler* consists of a controlled-for-financial-growth number of first and other editions, and one artist's proof. The pages are printed on high-quality pH opinion-neutral paper that meets all archival standards. The artist's proof has been hand printed on papyrus made from marsh grasses gathered near Buck's duck hunting blind. This proof is often used to decoy young hens wearing tank tops into the drink decoys strategically placed about the Valhalla Lounge on the arcade level of Buck's Duck Hunting Lodge, overlooking Big Babe Lake in northernmost Minnesota.

The publisher certifies that this signature edition was produced from the original papyrus edition and has been personally inspected by Buck while reloading. The printing plates are in the safe custody (well, er, actually, they're hidden behind the hard-boiled eggs on the back bar). Should the plates be destroyed to artificially inflate the retail value of those copies sold in the United States, there is more than a little reason to suspect that Buck will issue a contraband edition in Canada, solely for financial gain. The larger literary considerations are another matter.